Emotional Abuse Recovery

Men & Women Suffering in Silence – Emotionally Abusive, Destructive Relationship or Marriage with Manipulative, Toxic People (Healthy Healing and Recovering from Trauma)

Marjorie Lise

an illegal act regardless of the end form the information ultimately takes. This includes copied versions of the work both physical, digital and audio unless express consent of the Publisher is provided beforehand. Any additional rights reserved.

Furthermore, the information that can be found within the pages described forthwith shall be considered both accurate and truthful when it comes to the recounting of facts. As such, any use, correct or incorrect, of the provided information will render the Publisher free of responsibility as to the actions taken outside of their direct purview. Regardless, there are zero scenarios where the original author or the Publisher can be deemed liable in any fashion for any damages or hardships that may result from any of the information discussed herein.

Additionally, the information in the following pages is intended only for informational purposes and should thus be thought of as universal. As befitting its nature, it is presented without assurance regarding its prolonged validity or interim quality. Trademarks that are mentioned are done without written consent and can in no way be considered an endorsement from the trademark holder.

Table of Contents

Your Free Resource Is Awaiting

To better help you, I've created a simple mind map you can use _right away_ to easily understand, quickly recall and readily use what you'll be learning in this book.

Click Here To Get Your Free Resource

Alternatively, here's the link:

https://viebooks.club/freeresourcemindmapforemotionalabuserecovery

Introduction

This book is meant to help everybody. While it looks at abuse from a more feminine light, it can and will help people of both sexes. Be warned, there will be examples of abuse in this book. These examples are by no means considered to be true stories, and if they do contain similarities to your life or somebody you know, it is by coincidence only. It may, in the end, help you to relate better to my book.

I will also be drawing on personal experience in the realm of emotional abuse. It is something that has touched my life deeply. Through my journey, I have found ways that I feel will help others, and I will share some personal stories later on.

Emotional abuse, typically in the form of verbal abuse, is a battering for which there are no physical bruises, yet it is just as painful, and recovery tends to take a lot longer. When you live as a victim of abuse, your life becomes increasingly confusing. While in public, your abuser acts like one person, and then behind closed doors, they become somebody else.

Oftentimes, there is no other witness for the abused person and nobody else to understand what you have gone through. What's worse is other people in your life may see the abuser as a nice guy, which is what he sees himself as.

Like I said earlier, while many examples come from the woman's perspective, it is a fact that men also suffer emotional abuse. But, in the end, there is a difference. When talking about adult emotionally abusive relationships, if a man is a victim, they tend not to live in the same type of fear as female victims do. As for emotional abuse that occurs in childhood, both sexes' experiences tend to be similar.

This book is made to help you notice the subtle signs of emotional abuse. I want to reveal the slight nuances and reality that this type of abuse can cause. Everybody who has experienced emotional abuse would much rather forget their past altogether. Everybody would love to forget the bad parts of their past, but we can't. What we can do is learn from those times and make choices now to make sure we have a better future.

If you do decide, or already know, that you have been a victim of emotional abuse, I hope this book will lead you in the right direction for recovery.

Part I: Emotional Abuse

Chapter 1: What is Emotional Abuse

Emotional abuse doesn't discriminate. It can happen to anybody: adults, teens, or children. Even adults who had a good childhood with a solid foundation can find themselves in an emotionally abusive relationship. Once a person has become free from the abuse, they are then able to realize that something was wrong. While they are still enduring the trauma, it can be hard to see that they have other options.

Just because no physical marks are left behind doesn't mean that there isn't a problem or that a crime wasn't committed. The main thing this means is that law enforcement isn't as willing to help you when you need it.

Due to this "problem," emotional abuse is quite elusive. While it has a tendency to be invisible to the outside world, emotional abuse has the ability to carve out deep wounds in a person's mind. The problems that this causes can fester and turn into bigger problems over the years, which cause more emotional problems that can bubble to the surface in many ways. Getting out of the relationship doesn't always stop the abuse.

People who have suffered through abuse but don't properly address it and release the emotional baggage can push these issues onto their children. If it stays suppressed, it can cause emotional harm to turn into a disease that can be passed down. People may end up finding themselves lashing out at others, not knowing how to communicate and not understanding love. Before long, you could end up scarring your own children because of some unaddressed issues you didn't know you had.

Therefore, if you have been subjected to emotional abuse, it is crucial that you learn what it is, why it has happened, and how you can overcome it. No matter how hard this might be to spot and fix, you must do this for your health and for the health of generations to come.

Definition of Emotional Abuse

In psychological texts, emotional abuse is defined as an action that diminishes, isolates, humiliates, confines, and verbally assaults a person's self-worth, dignity, and identity. This is a form of chronic psychological abuse that can lead to anxiety, low self-confidence, personality changes, depression, and even suicide. [1]

People who emotionally abuse others will use a person's emotions to mess with their mind and make them bow to their wishes. Like verbal abuse, emotional abuse isn't spotted during the early stages, so the ramifications for victims compound as the abuse continues. If a victim can spot the early signs, they are more likely to seek help.

While it is very important to spot emotional abuse, there are certain times when things aren't actually considered abuse. Since this type of abuse is so hard to spot, knowing the types of scenarios that don't fall into the abuse category can help people to notice the difference between abusive and non-abusive behaviors.

People sometimes lump certain life experiences into the category of emotional abuse, but most aren't. Things like breakups, arguments, divorces, and being brutally honest with somebody when it is in response to a question is not actual emotional abuse. Yes, these things can cause varying degrees of pain and stress, but they are not abuse.

If you and your partner are having an argument, you have to look at the situation and find the cause of the argument. If the two of you actually have a concrete issue that has created this argument, then this is just a normal human interaction because all disagreements can't be avoided. Furthermore, if you have asked a person for their honest opinion and they give it to you, there is a chance you won't like it, but it doesn't constitute abuse. These are just hard realities of life that everybody has to face.

There are many other insistences in life where the line of abuse gets blurry. For instance, yelling normally plays a big part in emotional abuse, yet just because somebody yells doesn't mean they are being abusive. People yell at each other sometimes to make a point, or because they are experiencing a moment of anger, or because they care. What differentiates these moments from actual abuse is that once you have had your outburst, you both sit down and take some time to talk about your differences. This helps the hurt that somebody may have experienced to dissipate.

Another important bit of information when it comes to yelling is the object of the outburst. If another person is yelling about something you did or an issue between the two of you, they are merely expressing some dissatisfaction. But, if they are shouting deliberately hurtful words at you, this is getting closer to abuse. For example, my husband forgot about a date night we were supposed to have the other week. He came home so late that we missed the concert we were supposed to go to, and I ended up yelling about it. After I had calmed down, we both talked it out; he apologized and made it up to me. Now, on the other hand, had I screamed things at him like, "You're an idiot," "You're a jackass for forgetting out date," or "You mess up everything," then I would be verging on abuse.

It's important that you learn how to differentiate between an expression of emotion and a verbal assault. This is the difference between an intention to express a viewpoint and an intention to harm.

Another way to help you understand the difference between abusive and non-abusive behavior is how often the action occurs. Let's take a look at some examples:

- If your significant other raises their voice and gets upset about once every four months or so, this isn't abusive behavior. If they yell because they get angry at you every single day, this is abusive.

- Let's say your significant other just lost their job and they come home upset and express this in a physical manner on a random object, this isn't abuse. If they are constantly in a rage and breaking things, this is abusive.

As you can tell, there are some behaviors that are normal and some that are abusive depending on their occurrence. As we continue through the book, you will find it easier to spot the things that happen too often and cross the line. For now, understanding how often an action occurs has a large impact on if it is abusive behavior.

Abuse will also often involve intimidation, so when it comes to verbal threats, they are almost always a sign of emotional abuse. Overall, the goal of the abuse is to control and undermine a person while an upset loved one is just looking to address the problem that upset them.

Emotional abuse is very much an umbrella term and includes any abusive act that does not include physical abuse. Since it is a broad term, it can include many different abusive behaviors that can damage a person's mental state. Emotional abuse does follow the same cycle that physical abuse follows. Once the victim starts to realize that they are being abused, the abuser will start to change up their actions, temporarily, to guilt the victim into believing they made a mistake. [2]

It is also common for the emotionally abusive person to not realize they are being abusive. Instead, they often feel insecure about whether or not their partner actually likes them, so they feel like they have to constantly check in on them or blame them for things they likely didn't do. The constant checking in, blame, and accusations are all types of emotional abuse. [2]

They may believe that they know what is best for the other person or what looks best to the outside world, so they try to control their partner's every move. They criticize their partner when they don't do something the right way. They also get very defensive if their partner argues with them because that is evidence that they don't have as much control as they would like to believe. They can criticize how they walk, talk, dress, and interact with others. [2]

Emotional Abuse Examples

Let's take a look at which actions actually constitute emotional abuse.

- A sign of abuse is when a person intentionally threatens violence, frightens, abandons, or causes fear of proper care or no food.

- Lying to another person or asking another person to lie is also a sign of abuse.

- Socially isolating a person is abuse.

- If important information is hidden, other information is fabricated, and any other form slander and defamation is used, that is abuse.

- Bringing up the subject of death to try and get somebody to do something, like "I will kill myself if you don't stay with me," is emotionally abusive.

- Telling a person they aren't worth the trouble or are too much trouble is abuse, as is criticizing or ignoring them.

- Trying to force a person to comply with unreasonable demands, treating a child as a servant, or treating an adult like a child is abusive.

There are a lot of different ways in which emotional abuse can manifest itself, and these are only a few of the main behaviors that you can start to look for. Remember, emotional abuse isn't obvious, and people tend to have a blind spot when it comes to family and friends. We tend to make excuses for others that keep us in an abusive situation.

Here's an example you might be able to connect with:

Eileen is constantly criticizing Brad in the hope that by belittling him, she can control how he acts. She cuts him down when they are together and belittles him in front of friends. Whenever he tries to say something, she tries to make him out to be the crazy one, like nobody ever takes him seriously. She says he is the cause for her unhappiness, holding him responsible for her feelings. She refuses to take responsibility for how she behaves and acts. She also keeps a double-standard when it comes to how she acts, not holding herself to the same standards that she holds him to.

Eileen puts him down with words like dumb, inept, and stupid. When he talks to her friends and family, she constantly rolls her eyes to try to get them to disrespect him as well. She often treats him with disgust and disdain. She will often threaten to leave. She won't show him any affection unless he does exactly what she tells him to. When mad, she is often nonverbal. She has even gone days without talking to him. Eileen also crosses the line and talks to Brad's family and friends behind his back, isolating him from people who might be supportive and help him. Eileen shows a distinct abusive pattern that hits Brad at different angles.

Emotional abuse is just as serious, if not more so, as physical abuse. The main purpose of the abuse is to control others.

Chapter 2: Forms of Emotional Abuse

Once you have gotten accustomed to spotting the traits and characteristics of the emotionally abusive person, it will become easy to spot them. You will also start to notice that you feel drained when you have been around them. This chapter is going to help teach you about the different traits, characteristics, and types of emotional abuse.

Psychological abuse can be found everywhere. It can happen amongst friends, at work, at college, in relationships, and in family life. You can't escape it. These abusers are out there and it's very hard to avoid them. But it is possible to identify them from the way they act. This is the reason why it is so important to be on the alert and to understand how to interpret what could be their actual intentions. These abusive people are also known as toxic people. They are draining and hard to deal with and leave you feeling used.

Scholars and psychologists aren't totally sure how to evaluate them because these abusers are far from suffering from a mental illness. In the majority of cases, they create damage by using the power they have over others.

There are many red flags to help warn you and make sure that you don't get trapped by another emotionally abusive person. The first things we are going to look at are these warnings.

1. Verbal Put-Downs

The emotional abuser loves to put their partner down, especially in public, so that they can cause them the most embarrassment.

2. Cruelty

Most emotional abusers lack empathy for people, animals, or their partner. They are only concerned about themselves. If they aren't being hurt, then they could care less.

3. Isolates Their Victim

One of the first things that an abuser will do is to isolate their partner from their closest friends and family. It can be as drastic as physically moving them away or by making it extremely difficult to see others.

4. Wants to Believe They are Perfect

Emotional abusers refuse to accept flaws in others, so they aren't going to want to think that they are anything less than perfect. They work very hard to show off to everybody else that they are perfect, but if you take a closer look, you will start to see all the cracks in the façade. Their image and their work are all smoke and mirrors.

They act according to their own beliefs. They don't think about other people's views. They impose their ideas on others no matter the context. When it comes to disagreements, they won't budge because their views have to be accepted. An emotional abuser believes that they master every situation and are always right. Everybody else is wrong and opinions different than their own are wrong.

5. Control over the Finances

Making sure that they have complete control of all the money that comes into the home is a great way to keep a person right where you want them. Not allowing them to work and keeping the money keeps the victim under their thumb.

6. Moody

It's draining when you don't know what kind of mood your partner is going to be in, but it can also cause anxiety. It can also cause the victim to try harder to please their partner so that they are in a good mood.

These abusers are the types of people who aren't all that great at managing their emotions. When they don't succeed, they find that it is very hard for them to start over. If they do succeed, they think they did it all on their own. Both extremes are bad, but the emotional abuser loves going to extremes. They don't have self-criticism, but they are great at superficially judging themselves. They can end up becoming depressed. This is because they have low self-esteem, even if they don't want to show it.

7. They Start out Helpful and Charming

A common theme you will find in adults who were in romantic relationships with their abuser is that they were confident and charming when they first met. It made others gravitate towards them.

While working to gain the trust of their victims, they act like the nicest person on Earth. This makes it hard for other people to figure out their real intentions. Their charisma sucks people in and everywhere they go, others love them. Even once their mask comes off and they start to show their true self, others refuse to believe that they are abusive. The victim's disappointment can be so great at times that some people never accept the truth.

8. Childish

While emotional abusers may start out charming, if they don't get what they want, they will start to act childish. They love to make unreasonable demands and then manage to make you wonder what you messed up.

9. They Have Problems They Ignore

It is common knowledge that someone who abuses others does this because they suffered through trauma at some point in their life. When people are able to confront these things, they will become healthier. It can become very dangerous when a person refuses to accept the fact that something is wrong with them, not only for them, but everybody else in their life.

10. You Get Blamed for Their Unhappiness

If you hadn't gone out, if you didn't look at the girl at the mall, if only they were your first and only, so on and so forth. The abuser will find anything and everything to blame you for but never face their own actions.

11. Extremely Jealous

Jealousy is one of the main signs of insecurity. Their subconscious is always asking "Why are they with me?" Their conscious mind, on the other hand, is warning them that their significant other is flirting with other people. Most of the time, they aren't actually flirting.

12. Judgmental Towards Others

The emotional abuser is quick to judge other people. Literally, anything can cause them to judge; the person went to the wrong school, they wear the wrong clothing, and they hang out with the wrong people. If the abuser views another person as some type of threat, they can't be around them.

They don't accept that other people have different views. Their world is the only thing that counts, and they don't care about anybody else. When they are in relationships with the opposite sex, they will often see their partner as inferior. They treat others the same way in which they have been treated. If they believe the way others believe, then they will talk. They allow themselves to be influenced by the prejudices of society. This is why they always discriminate and are disrespectful to people who are different than they are.

13. They Project a Perfect Image

An abuser's image can mean several things, and it may not even directly concern them. For example, their good image could mean that their kids are going to the best school or they made straight A's. As long as things in their life turn out good, they remain happy.

14. They Sulk a Lot

This ties into their childishness and follows the same pattern where the victim will start to see that it is easier to just try and make their abuser happy, so they start to modify their behavior. [3]

These are all great traits to help you spot an emotionally abusive person, but there are different types of emotional abuse. Let's take a look at those next.

Parental Abuse

This is probably a type of abuse that you don't want to think about, but it happens and is fairly common. This can include abuse from stepparents, guardians, grandparents, and anybody else that is a parental figure in a child's life. Here's an example: Grandma Jean came to visit and made some comments about her granddaughter, how fat she was looking and how she dresses. While the comments are infrequent and it might not seem like abuse at first, the derogatory statements are abuse. Grandma isn't doing much to help the child gain confidence; instead, she is taking it away from her.

Hurtful and offhanded comments, like the ones from the example, are just one instance where abuse doesn't actually require a pattern from a single person. Children tend to be more sensitive to things like this, and they leave a lasting impression when they happen over a long period of time and on a regular basis. In fact, the more people that say a certain thing to a child, the more it will affect them.

Constant negative comments aimed towards different personality traits from physical appearance to behavior have a lasting impression on a child. While it's sad how frequently this abuse happens between parents and children, what's worse is the complicated reason behind the abuse. Parents who berate their child with the reason for causing harm are disturbed people. Chances are, though, the parent doesn't actually hate their child. Their hurtful remarks are likely due to incompetence.

For example, if a child is a little heavier or they have developed a few unhealthy habits, their parent's comments could be their warped way of expressing their concern about their wellbeing. This is ineffective and harmful, but, unfortunately, harshness and insults are the only things that some people understand. There's actually a good chance that the parents were raised with these types of insults as well. [3]

Here are a few of the most common examples of parental emotional abuse:

1. Calling their child anorexic or fat.

2. Ignoring their child.

3. Telling their child that they are stupid or aren't going to amount to anything.

4. Controlling the things that a child is allowed to say or do, without a good reason. For example, being forceful with their child and not letting them express their own thoughts and feelings if they aren't what the parents what to hear.

5. Taunting their child.

6. Isolating their child from their other parent or never allowing the two to be together.

7. Not letting their child go to a friend's house because they don't like a friend or their parents. This combines isolation with other emotional abuse traits.

8. Telling their child that their grades are bad when they aren't.

This likely has you all wondering where parenting fits into things. Where is the line drawn between abuse and a strict parent? First off, discipline is important in a child's life. The right kind of discipline can create a strong character and teaches right from wrong. To positively discipline a child, you have to teach them to respect rules and have strong values, a sense of morality, and a strong work ethic. Well-disciplined children are safer in the world as adults.

For some parents, strict parenting means creating a rigid daily routine for all their activities. Providing a child with a no-budge schedule is most often considered strict, but it isn't abuse. Discipline becomes abusive when the consequences and punishment from infractions turn inconsistent, excessive, and focused on causing fear instead of providing them a lesson.

Abusive parents won't think much about how they discipline their child and the punishments that they inflict will often be on a whim. Rather than explaining what they did wrong, the punishments are outbursts and little more than psychological torture or deprivation. The most common feature of an abusive home environment is unpredictability.

Here are two examples of two different home environments, one of which involves strict parenting and another of which is abusive:

Carol is a single parent to her thirteen-year-old son, William. Because she works but also wants to make sure that William succeeds, she has him follow a specific schedule every weekday that involves going to school followed by either after-school tutoring or basketball practice, depending on the day of the week and time of year. These activities always end at five, and William then goes to his father's house nearby for dinner and does his homework until his mother picks him up at seven. William knows that so long as he sticks to this schedule, he won't be in trouble. If he blows off one of his after-school activities or arrives at his father's house more than twenty minutes late, he will get his video games taken away for a week. He also knows that if his grades slip below a C average, his mother will start to worry and sit him down to talk about it, possibly even arrange for extra tutoring on Saturdays. She will also let his father know so that they can talk and see if there's a problem that William won't talk about with her. If she finds out it's because he's been slacking off, he won't be allowed to go to friends' houses on the weekend until his grades improve.

In this scenario, Carol has set up rigid schedule for William because she wants to be sure that she can keep William safe and on the right path even though she's a working single parent. It's all done with William's best interests at heart. William knows what is expected of him and what will happen if he doesn't do it. She is disciplined to teach him a lesson about not skipping out on his commitments or to instill a good work ethic, not to make him fear her. The no-budge schedule might seem strict, but it is not abusive.

Michelle is also a single working mother to her thirteen-year-old son, Charlie. Charlie never knows from one day to the next what to expect from his mother's rules. Even though she's rarely ever home by the time he gets home from school, he doesn't know when she'll be in a bad mood and yell at him for "coming home late." She never lets him participate in after-school activities, and there are very few friends that she'll let him spend time with at their houses because she doesn't like them and/or their parents. Even though his father lives nearby and Charlie wants to spend time with him, Michelle never lets Charlie see him, even making him stay home alone rather than go over to his house. Charlie's grades never slip below a B average, but he never knows when she'll scold him for "only" getting an A-.

In this situation, Michelle disciplines Charlie based on her own emotions, not what's best for him. She isolates him from his friends, his classmates, and his father, to the point of even leaving him alone rather than allowing him to interact with others. She belittles his achievements randomly and for seemingly no reason. Charlie doesn't know what to expect from his mother from one day to the next. Michelle is an emotionally abusive parent.

If your parents properly disciplined you, then you understood all their rules and if you didn't follow them, it was likely you already knew you were doing something wrong. Not only do the rules need to be clear, but the consequences should be, too. While each infraction should have a varying degree of punishment, a reward system for when their child acts well should also be in place. This encourages the child to behave well.

Relationship Abuse

Emotional abuse happens a lot between parent and child, but it also happens in other relationships with friends, spouses, or boyfriend/girlfriend. Most of the time, the person being abused isn't new to it. They likely faced emotional abuse as a child.

Let's not forget that men can be the victim as well. TV, movies, social media, and the like like to put emphasis on women being abused. It's important to make sure women get help, but something we don't see a lot of is how men are susceptible to being emotionally abused. Society has conditioned us to believe that men are always strong and never bullied, but it happens more than we know.

The problem is, though, a man being emotionally abused by a woman is more stigmatized than physical abuse. This is why most men won't report psychological terror.

Female-specific spousal abuse isn't all that different from male-specific. The one thing women tend to do more than a man is use sex as a weapon of control. In some extreme cases, the woman might threaten the man with accusations of rape.

I'm by no means trying to lessen what women face; I just want to shed some light on the other side of the story. When this type of abuse starts in a marriage, it tends to begin with one spouse trying to make things easier, and this causes them to isolate themselves.

Besides the common forms of control, men are more capable of causing specific types of emotional abuse. This is especially true for inflicting fear and threats of violence.

Both men and women, when abusive, will belittle, humiliate, and withhold affection from their partner. They try to control the relationships their partners have outside of the marriage as well. This type of behavior can last for years. Only when one spouse moves on or is pushed too far do they realize that trauma has taken place.

The most common cause of spousal abuse is a broken home. This isn't true for all, but it is common. The abuse is not your fault, and an important step in healing is to instill this truth in your mind. It's easy to become complacent, to just accept what is going on, and believe you can't do anything to change it, but you can stop it and heal.

Now, marriage isn't the only place emotional abuse can happen. It can occur in any relationships. This tends to be harder to notice, but then something changes within the relationship.

When it comes to abusive friendships, a lot of people underestimate how damaging the abuse can be. The reason for this is because friendships are viewed as things that can be easily disposed of more easily than marriages. True friends are not that common anymore and have turned into a wide circle of acquaintances. This means that friendships can be easily found but take years to build.

This is what makes misinterpreting an abusive friendship for a true friend so dangerous. The need for a friend causes a blind spot and leaves us holding onto a person who is only interested in using you for personal gain. They are nice when they need something, but it changes when you become less useful. This type of tainted friendship can happen to anybody, especially those who are considered "social butterflies."

Just because you may not be socially active doesn't mean that you have to settle for a person who belittles you and calls you names. Plus, it's a truth of life that it is better to be alone than be with a person who abuses you. This might sound harsh, but you'll find more success once you stop allowing yourself to be used by others who don't care about you. You will then start to attract those who actually care. [4]

Rejecting

A common trait of people who are emotionally abusive is rejecting their victim. A partner, parent, friend, or caregiver who displaces this type of behavior toward another will let their victim know, in different ways, that they aren't wanted. Belittling a person or putting down their worth are some ways that this type of emotional abuse manifests. Other types of rejecting can include telling a person to leave or, worse, calling them names, making them a scapegoat, or blaming them for other people's problems. Refusing to hold a child as they are growing or refusing to talk to another person is also abusive behaviors.

Ignoring

Adults who haven't really had their emotional needs met will find it hard to respond to the needs of others, especially their own children. They may not be able to attach to others or they can't provide a positive nurturing experience for their child. They might not show any interest in a person, or they withhold affection, or might not even acknowledge that another person is present. They are likely physically there, but they are completely emotionally unavailable. Failing to respond to another is emotional abuse.

Terrorizing

People who curse, yell, and threaten their child, spouse, or friend is doing serious psychological damage. Now, we talked about yelling earlier. Yelling and cursing are fine if it is temporary and the cause of it is addressed and you have a healthy conversation about what made them upset. Cursing and yelling AT another person constantly or for no reason is where it becomes abuse.

Singling out a person and ridiculing them for normal emotional reactions is abusive. Threatening a person with abandonment, physical harm, harsh words, or in severe cases, death, is completely unacceptable. Even if you are joking, causing a person to be terrified by intimidation or threats is some of the worst emotional abuse. When it comes to children, this includes knowing, hearing, or witnessing abuse within the home.

Isolating

This is a common abuse tactic by parents. When parents use isolation, they may not let their child engage in normal activities with their peers. They may keep a baby in their room, unexposed to external stimulation, or they can prevent their teen from participating in extracurricular activities. Requiring somebody to stay in their room from the time they get home from school until they go to school the next day, restricting what they eat, or forcing them to stay away from friends and family can be very destructive, depending on the severity and circumstances.

I didn't realize until later in life the damage my dad had done, which ended up leading me into an abusive marriage. He often tried to isolate me. My mom tried her best to find a happy medium between us, but he still held the reins. It was a hit and miss whether or not I got to participate in normal child activities. I had to make sure to ask at the right times for things or make sure I asked way in advance. For example, if a friend asked me on Wednesday or Thursday to spend the night on Friday, it wouldn't be enough notice for me to ask my dad. I didn't get to go to parties my friends threw because my dad thought they were a waste of time. Even though I was in the school band, it took an act of congress to get him to let me go to competitions. These are just a few of the examples of him isolating me.

Corrupting

People who are corruptive to others may allow their child to partake in drugs or alcohol or may enable the user. They talk others into treating animals cruelly or participate in criminal activities like gambling, prostitution, assault, stealing, and so on. Parents who are abusive might let their children watch inappropriate content for their age. Encouraging others to do things that are harmful or illegal is abusive and needs to be reported.

Exploiting

Exploitation is often considered manipulation or forcing an activity without considering the needs of others. For instance, if a parent were to constantly ask an eight-year-old child to be in charge of making dinner for the family is not appropriate. Giving somebody responsibilities that are bigger than a person can handle or using a person for profit is wrong.

Emotional Blackmail

Emotional blackmail has become very common in people. This trait of emotional abuse will cause the victims to feel vulnerable. Relationships have the ability to enhance a person's self-esteem or destroy it. A person who is close to you has the ability to be a threat because they are aware of your weaknesses and can use emotional blackmail to get things from you. As a victim, you will ultimately succumb to the guilt, obligation, and fear. This is why it helps when you can identify the signs of emotional blackmail.

People with insecurities often use emotional blackmail. They work by manipulating your decisions by responding in a negative way to what you do. They will try to intimidate you until you do the things that they want you to. These are clear warning signs of emotional blackmail. They will often accuse or blame you of doing things they don't like. They also won't hesitate to create drama when in public.

Emotional blackmailers will often use the Fear-Emotion-Guilt tactic. They start out with rage to confuse the victim and make them fearful. They will then slyly use their victim's emotions and sensibilities to make them look wrong. The victim's sentiments are used to divert their attention from truths to cause them to become an emotional mess.

Once they spot that you have let your guard down, they fill you with guilt. If you don't end up defending yourself, you will fall for their manipulation. Even if you have never done anything wrong to them, you will feel guilty and apologize for whatever has happened.

Gaslighting

Emotional abusers will try to make their victim feel like an idiot. They say things like, "It's all in your head" or "You sometimes have a bad memory, are you sure?" Gaslighting happens slowly in a relationship. In fact, the actions of the abuser will seem harmless at first. Over time, this behavior will continue and the victim will become depressed, isolated, anxious, and confused, while simultaneously losing their sense of reality.

People who gaslight will withhold things, refusing to listen or understand their partner. They counter their partner by asking them questions about their memory of events, even when they know their victim has remembered things correctly.

They like to divert the topic as well. If they don't want to talk about something, they will quickly change the subject. They will also trivialize their victim's feelings to make them feel unimportant.

They also deny and "forget" things in order to make themselves right. If they made a promise to their victim but they don't want to keep it, they

will often play it off as the victim making something up.

Some of the most common symptoms of gaslighting abuse are:

- You start wondering if you are "good enough."

- You feel like you can't do anything right.

- You feel joyless and hopeless.

- You feel like you used to be a different person, more relaxed, fun-loving, and confident.

- You can't make simple decisions.

- You start to lie so that you can avoid reality twists and put-downs.

- You feel like something is wrong, but you can't quite put your finger on it.

- You start to withhold information from family and friends so that you don't have to explain yourself.

- You make up a lot of excuses for the way your partner acts.

- You aren't able to understand why, with so many good things in life, that you aren't happy.

- You find that you are constantly apologizing to your partner.

- You feel confused or crazy.

- You start asking yourself why you are so sensitive.

- You are constantly second-guessing yourself. [5]

Chapter 3: Narcissistic, Socio-pathic, and Psychopathic Abuse

I have talked about emotional and psychological abuse and toxic people in general, but now I'm going to look into three very specific kinds of emotional abuse: narcissistic abuse, sociopathic abuse, and psychopathic abuse.

All emotional abuse is damaging, and if it goes too far, it can be life-threatening. By the time I was finally able to leave my ex, I was growing more and more concerned that his threats to kill both of us weren't so hollow. However, it's important to be able to recognize narcissistic, sociopathic, and psychopathic abuse because of their severity. While my abuse was severe, I have never had to deal with these forms of abuse, but I have talked with a few women who have. At least when it came to the sociopathic and psychopathic abus-ers, they felt lucky to make it out alive.

The difference among these kinds of abuse doesn't actually come from the abuse itself. It comes from the abusers. Anyone can be emotionally abusive—sometimes without even realizing it—without falling under any of these categories, but when they do, especially if they are psychopathic, there is an extra layer of lack of care and empathy for the victim. Mostly, though, these forms of abuse are defined by the motivation behind them. (I'll talk more about why people control other people in the chapter "Avoid and Remove Abusers".)

Narcissistic Abuse

Narcissistic abuse comes as a form of projection and deflection. Whichever way the abuser feels deficient, they'll project that onto their victims. For example, if the abuser is feeling unattractive, they might tell their victim that their outfit makes them look fat or that their new haircut looks horrible.

Or maybe the narcissist is feeling stupid because of some mistakes they made while paying the bills. The next time that they go out to dinner and their partner messes up calculating the tip, the narcissist might sneer at them, "Good going, Einstein." When their partner takes offense, they'll double down and say, "I was just teasing. Geez, where's your sense of humor?"

Similarly, if their victim tries to call them out on their behavior or in any way implies that the narcissist has a flaw, the abuser will deflect it back onto the victim. For example, if the victim is trying to confront the abuser about embarrassing them in front of friends, they'll turn it around and say something like, "What are you talking about? Why do you always have to do this in front of our friends?"

- Malignant Narcissist

  Narcissists who are particularly malicious are known as malignant narcissists. They aren't bothered by the emotional abuse they inflict on their victims. In fact, some of them enjoy it. They can be sadistic and find joy in hurting others. Still, at their core, the malignant narcissist's abusive behavior comes from a toxic combination of an inflated sense of self-importance and a fragile self-esteem.

You can learn more about narcissists and daughters' relationships with their narcissistic mothers in ***Did My Narcissistic Mother Love Me?*** by Nanette Abigail.

Sociopathic and Psychopathic Abuse

There's a fine line between sociopaths and psychopaths—and, as a result, between sociopathic and psychopathic abuse. The words are often used interchangeably in everyday conversation. Regardless, there is a difference.

In an article written for *Psychology Today* called "The Difference Between Sociopathy and Psychopathy", Kristen Fuller, M.D., both are clinically classified as Antisocial Personality Disorder (ASPD). They have no regards for the rules of society or other people's rights.

However, Fuller goes on to note that sociopaths are impulsive and prone to bouts of rage. Psychopaths, on the other hand, are cold, calculating, and expertly manipulative. Most importantly, sociopaths can and do form emotional bonds to people. Psychopaths cannot. They have absolutely no empathy whatsoever and use people with no remorse.

Due to the shared disregard for the rules of society and other people's rights, sociopathic and psychopathic abuse stem from the same psychological root: they only care about their own wants and needs. They want the control over their victims as a means to make their ends meet, and they don't give much thought to how it will affect the victims—or they do and simply don't care.

Psychopathic abuse is generally more dangerous for the victim than sociopathic abuse. While a sociopath is more likely to lose their temper than a psychopath, a sociopath will also be more likely to feel some level of empathy for their victim. The psychopath will emotionally abuse their victim guilt-free and without fear of losing a bond they have not formed with the other person. All they care about is what they can gain from the abuse: control over you, control over other people's opinions of you, possibly joy at your expense.

I've learned over years of interacting with other abuse survivors that sociopathic and psychopathic abuse are much less common than other forms of emotional abuse. However, if you are currently in such a situation or find yourself in one in the future, you will find that the advice in this book applies as much to narcissistic, sociopathic, and psychopathic abuse as to others. They might have different causes and are potentially more dangerous, but these are all still kinds of emotional abuse. Just remember, as always, to proceed with caution and put your own safety first.

Chapter 4: The Emotional Abuse Victim

The abuser has their reason for doing what they do, and victims have a reason for ending up in these types of relationships. We're going to take a look at the characteristics of a victim as well as how they feel.

While low self-esteem and previous abuse are likely risk factors for being a victim, anybody can end up being abused. Fear, shock, or embarrassment for a child's wellbeing might cause a victim to stay in an abusive relationship. Here are some common characteristics of victims of abuse:

1. Quick Involvement

They have probably been hurt in prior relationships, or they don't feel like they are good enough to be loved for who they are. They suffer from low self-esteem. They find it hard to protect themselves, and if another person pays them some attention, they have to give in to whatever they want because they might be the last person to marry.

2. Lack Self-Care

People who have been abused will often have behaviors that present possible health risks, like
sexual promiscuity, eating disorders, cutting
themselves, suicide attempts, alcoholism, and
substance abuse. The more severe the abuse they
go through, the greater the chance is that they
abuse themselves. They will likely feel guilty
when they nurture themselves or act in ways that
suit their benefits. They give to other people instead of making sure they are taken care of.

3. Often a Perfectionist

Victims will often have very high standards that
normally can't be attained, and they will get upset
when they can't reach them. They will cover up
their poor views of themselves by being angry,
bitter, manipulative, or controlling.

4. Burdened and Serious

Victims typically have a hard time having fun, especially if they didn't have a healthy childhood.
Think about the fear a person has to feel every day
when they constantly have to tell reasons for the

behaviors, decisions, and whereabouts. Constant hope for a happy relationship that never happens and being criticized for everything they do drains the joy out of them.

5. Impulsive

A victim will often take on a decisive role without thinking about what it means or considering other alternatives. Because they can't make their own decisions, there are times when they will make unwise and rapid decisions because they haven't practiced using their own volition. There are times when they end up confused or feel victimized by those around them.

6. Hopelessness and Helplessness

Feelings of unfounded guilt, shame, control, isolation, and denial can be held over from family or past abusive experiences. This will result in feelings of helplessness and hopelessness. The only way they view themselves is as a failure because they have been taught that nothing they do is good. They think that they can't do anything right, and these beliefs are reinforced by the abuser. They believe that they don't have any control or power over their life or other external events that might negatively impact them.

7. Denies Feelings

They will repress, minimize, or deny feelings that could have occurred as a result of painful relationships or a traumatic childhood. They may not know the impact of their inability to express feelings and how it has impacted their lives. They find it hard to maintain intimate relationships and will describe themselves as numb.

8. Dependent

They are often very dependent and are terrified of being abandoned, so they keep themselves in relationships and situations that could harm them. Their dependency and fears keep them from ending unfulfilled relationships and keeps them from getting into fulfilling ones. Since they feel unlovable, it's hard, if not impossible, for them to believe that a person could actually love them for who they are. They will do everything possible to please others, hoping that they will be good enough to be loved. They can't define a healthy relationship in which their needs will be met as well.

9. Controlling

A victim feels the need to be in control. Abusers keep them focused on trivial needs like meals, the clothing they wear, or the rules in the house. The victim hopes that if they control these things, then they won't be abused. When the abuser does criticize them, they will feel like they didn't do something right and end up becoming more controlling. They will overreact to the slightest bit of change, especially with things that they can't control.

10. Co-Dependent

Victims have a hard time with commitment, trust, security, and intimacy in relationships. Since their abuser has made their focus be on their abuser's wishes, requirements, and needs, the victim loses sight of who they are. Without defined personal boundaries and limits, they become enmeshed with their partner's erratic behavior and needs so much so they start justifying their abusive actions.

11. Irresponsible or Responsible to Extremes

They like to take responsibility for solving other people's problems or they expect others to be responsible for fixing theirs. This isn't at all surprising considering that their abuser tells them that his actions are their fault. They could end up waiting for somebody else to save them from an abusive relationship. This allows them to avoid being responsible for their choices and actions.

12. Blaming

Victims also like to blame others for their own circumstances and often find themselves attracted to those who are controlling or who take charge. They will confuse love and pity and likes those who they think they can rescue or take care of. Because they need to feel loved, they view their abuser's dependency as love.

13. Seeks Acceptance, Recognition, Affirmation, and Approval

They are desperate to find approval, affirmation, acceptance, and love, and they will do anything to make others like them. They don't want to hurt others, so they stay loyal in relationships and situations even when it can easily be seen that loyalty isn't deserved. This causes them to attract emotionally unavailable people who have an addictive personality.

14. Harshly Judges Themselves

They perpetuate the negative messages that they hear from their abusers and judge themselves, as well as others, based on those beliefs without even thinking that the beliefs could be wrong. Since they have isolated themselves from those who might give them positive messages, they only hear the negative views. This ends up causing them to feel hopeless.

15. Isolated

They feel they are alone and that nobody understands what is happening. They will often isolate themselves out of fear of upsetting their partner. They will feel awkward around others, especially authority figures or people with assertive personalities. While they have isolated themselves, they also fear abandonment and rejection. [3]

A Victim's Feelings

A victim will, most of the time, be aware of their feelings, but they are so controlled by their abusers, they let their abuser tell them how they feel. When it comes to getting out and healing, the victim's feelings are their best guides.

For example, when I was in the center of my abusive marriage, if I got upset about something, like normal people do sometimes, all my husband would say were things like, "You're taking this wrong" or "You're making a mountain out of a molehill." All he wanted to do was define my experience for me. He was explaining my reality. Before I realized what he was doing, I believed the things he said, and this caused a lot of confusion.

A person's feelings are very complex. Feelings aren't always easy to articulate or recognize. They are shaped by beliefs about our reality and ourselves, and they can be repressed. A person can use the energy of their feelings destructively or constructively.

Let's look at personal power. Let's say that we have reached a state of autonomy, integrity, serenity, and clarity. Here, we have purpose and meaning in our life. This is personal power. Now, if two people are in this state of being and are in a relationship with each other, this state becomes magnified. They are empowered together.

If one person in a relationship hasn't found their personal power, they will likely seek out power by controlling the other person. This will damage their partner's connection with themselves. The spirit ends up being diminished in this relationship.

Certain feelings harm the spirit like bruises harm the body. Certain feelings show the needs of the spirit. Certain feelings tell us the activity the spirit needs. This makes feelings indicators.

A victim will often feel responsible and inadequate. Responsibility nourishes the spirit while inadequacy harms the spirit. Victims feel responsible for everything and everyone, especially their abuser. That means when he's angry, she feels responsible for it. This means they feel responsible for their happiness, so when their abuser isn't happy, they feel inadequate.

A victim will feel affection and rejection. Affection feeds their spirit while rejection hurts the spirit. They want to express their love and affection for their partner, but these displays of affection are rejected by their partner. This ends up causing them to feel rejected and as if they have done something wrong. This rejection will end up breeding uncertainty and confusion.

They will often flip between hope and disappointment as well. The victim hopes that their relationship is going to get better. They probably see that communication is a bit difficult, but they hope that once they learn their partner enough, things will get easier. They continue to hope for these different things, but it never happens. When these hopes don't come true, the victim ends up filled with disappointment.

The victim ultimately ends up confused. The conflicting emotions that their partner shares confuses the victim because they can't fix them. Resolving the inner conflict is achieved once they realize they are being abused.

Chapter 5: The Actions of an Abuser

In this chapter, we are going to take a quick look at the abuser's reality and why they do what they do. As mentioned in the last chapter, the abuser has never known personal power, so they always work to overpower others. They reject their partner's openness and warmth because they fear these qualities.

In the reality that the abuser lives in, these emotions mean vulnerability. Vulnerability can end up leading to death. The abuser doesn't really think about the pain they are causing other people. The emotional abuser will minimize the abuse if called out on it, and they will express love in direct contrast to the negative things they have told their partner. In my experience and of others that I have spoken with, partners of abusers have heard at least two of the following declarations of love:

- All I want is for you to be happy.

- I would never hurt you.

- I'll never leave you.

- Nobody else could love you as I do.

- I love you.

In the abuser's reality, I love you means something very different than it does to others. I love you, to them, means grooming their partner to what they think they should be.

Keep in mind that everybody is different, and so are abusers. Some abusers are very demanding and overpowering. Others can be reclusive and are only demanding on occasion but are extremely manipulative. Some might always be angry. Some "hunt" in packs, while others are loners.

Emotional abusers can have all, many, or a few of the characteristics we are going to look at. By their nature, some of these characteristics are hard to recognize. The abuser will often describe themselves as the opposite of what their partner says. Emotional abusers can be:

- Frequently argumentative or demanding or uncommunicative and silent

- Controlling

- Unable to show empathy and warmth

- They diminish their partner's views and feelings

- Intense

- Angry

- Unpredictable

- Will blame their partner for their actions or outbursts

- Irritable

- Can't express their feelings

- Hostile

- Explosive

- Manipulative

- Critical

- Quick with put-downs and come-backs

- Jealous

- Sullen

- Competitive

Oftentimes, what is present in these abusive relationships shows what is lacking. Here are some examples:

- Inequality and Equality

Since abusers have to find power in others, they can't accept their partner as an equal. If they were to view their partner as an equal, then it will make them inferior. This would open them up to feelings and emotions that they don't want to experience.

A sure-fire way to spot inequality in a relationship is to see if the couple can create mutual goals and talk about them. With abusive relationships, couples can't plan together. Making plans requires them to be equal, and this doesn't exist in the abuser's reality. They can't even plan what they are going to do for the weekend. Here's an example:

Shirley thought it would be fun to visit a lake on Saturday. Friday evening, she asks, "Bruce, have you made any plans for tomorrow?"

Bruce angrily turns to her as replies, "Do I have to have plans?"

"No, I just thought we might do something together."

Even angrier, "I don't see why I must have plans."

"What are you upset about? I didn't say you had to have any plans."

"I'm not upset! Just forget about it!" Bruce screams, "You mentioned having plans and now you are trying to weasel out of them!"

This leaves Shirley feeling upset, frustrated, and confused. She doesn't understand how she can feel so bad while also not being able to talk about them. From past experiences, she knew that

Bruce would say that she was "trying to get out of the plans."

Shirley will spend some time wondering how she had upset Bruce. Had she caused him to feel like she expected him to have plans? When something like this happens, nobody is around to help Shirley sort things out.

- Competition and Partnership

An abuser is in constant competition with their partner, but they don't want their partner to contribute. Anything that their partner achieves is seen as a threat. Here's another story from a victim:

Sam was away on a business trip and Bella was taking care of the children. She decided to repaint the bathroom. Once Sam got home, she waited until after dinner to tell him what she had done. Bella took him to the bathroom and showed him. Instead of being happy, he replied with "You think you are the only person who works! I work, too!" She tried to assure him that wasn't how she felt, but he stayed angry. There was nothing she could say that would make him understand her intentions. This caused her to feel frustrated.

- Control and Intimacy

When the abuser refuses to talk about problems, they are preventing any chance of resolution. This is how they exercise control over their relationships. This leaves their partners feeling hurt because their feelings never find closure.

The emotional abuse closes all doors to true intimacy and communication. In order to be intimate, there has to be some form of mutuality, and this requires willingness to share, openness, and goodwill.

Cycle of Abuse

The cycle of abuse has five parts. Each abuser will have their own way of achieving each section, but the cycle will always work in the same way.

1. Gain Trust

First, they will gain the trust of the potential victim by being charming, loving, and attentive.

2. Over-involvement

The abuser starts to play a large role in the love of their victim. They start becoming involved in everything that the victim does and possibly dictating some of their actions.

3. Jealousy and Rules

They start to insert rules into their victim's life so that they can control their relationships. When the abuser acts out in jealousy, they view it as an act of love.

4. Control, Power, and Manipulation

The abuser starts blaming the victim for all their actions and behavior. The victim is then manipulated and coerced through the abuser's various tactics.

5. Traumatic Bonding

The continuing cycles of abuse will likely end up leading to a bond between the abuser and the victim.

Once the abuser has enacted their manipulation and coercion tactics, the victim might say something about their abuse, or they might not. Either way, the abuser will normally go back into the loving phase to ensure that the victim will not leave them. They will become very apologetic, woo the victim, present the victim with gifts and/or acts of kindness, anything that regains their trust. The victim starts to feel that the abuser won't do it again—might even doubt their own judgment in whether the original incident was as bad as they had thought—and everything starts over again.

Chapter 6: Effects of Emotional Abuse

A universal human need is to be understood and to understand. When you are in an abusive relationship, these needs are not met. The tricky part is that the victim has the rational thought that they can learn to understand their partner, which keeps them in the relationship.

The fact that they aren't able to understand their partner because of their abusive actions will defeat them through the power plays is incomprehensible to the victim. When they don't come to this realization, though, it leaves them in this incomprehensible reality where they are faced with the blame of their own battering.

Victims of this kind of abuse will slowly start to lose their self-esteem and confidence, most of the time without knowing it. This is what we are going to look at in this chapter. We're going to go through some of the consequences of emotional abuse. You are probably going to read some things in this chapter that you will resonate with, as well.

The victim of emotional abuse will likely experience:

- Distrust of future relationships.

- They live in the future, "I'll be happy when..."

- Believing that what they do best is actually what they do worst.

- A desire to escape.

- Reluctance to reach conclusions.

- Hesitant to accept their views.

- Desire not to be how they are, for example, too sensitive.

- Feeling as though time is flying by, but they are missing out on something.

- Fear of being crazy.

- Worried that they aren't as happy as they should be.

- Internalized critical voice.

- A growing sense of self-doubt.

- Loss of self-confidence.

- A want to soul-search and reviewing past experiences with the hope that they can figure out what happened.

- Worried that something is wrong with them.

- Uncertain as to how they come across.

- Constantly on-guard.

- Loss of enthusiasm.

- Distrust of their spontaneity.

Emotional abuse kills the spirit and removes life's joy. It changes the victim's reality because their abuser responds in a way that is odd for what is going on. The victim believes the abuser to be telling them the truth and can come up with a million reasons for what he says.

The victim is stuck living on hope. They cling to the moments where things seem normal, and they believe the upsets will slowly go away. A lot

of victims have said that their partners occasionally bought them things, complimented their
looks, and shared something personal. From time
to time, their expectations would grow, and they
would forget what their abuser had done. They
would hope for a better future, and it's this hope
that kept them in the relationship. [3]

We are going to take a look at an interaction that
shows the discrepancy in the communication that
leaves the partner confused.

Amy and James had three children, two of whom
were in college. On the outside, their marriage
looked great, but James had become more abusive over the years. Amy shared this story about
their relationship:

James called the house and asked to speak with
their daughter. Amy told him that she was taking
a shower and asked him if he wanted her to call
him back. He replied, "Yes," and said, "She called
me asking about the stereo. Let her know that I
don't know what's wrong." Amy replied, "Okay,
I'll let her know."

He then replied with, "No, I can call back later, or she can call when she gets the chance."

Amy said, "Okay, what message would you like me to give her?"

James came back full of rage, "I didn't ask you to write down a message!"

Amy was in pain and shock at his outburst. She was also trying to understand why he thought she thought that he had asked her to take a message. Everybody in their household would write down messages for each other. She had so many emotions going through her head that she could barely speak. She ended the call with, "I'll let her know you called, bye."

Amy spent the rest of the day thinking, "If I hadn't asked him his message, I wouldn't feel this way." She kept thinking she said something wrong and she now felt like dying. She had been thinking about going back to work, but now she was wondering if she could make it if she couldn't relate to her husband.

James never did things like this when there were other people around. While Amy tried to talk with her husband about the problems, he would always revert back to diverting, accusing, discounting, or denying.

Emotional abuse ends up leaving the victim confused and frustrated and can lead to depression and anxiety. One theory even suggests that emotional abuse could contribute to the development of chronic fatigue syndrome and fibromyalgia. [2] Emotional abuse, though hard to see, leaves indelible marks on its victims.

Effects on Victims of Childhood Emotional Abuse

Emotional abuse as an adult is traumatizing enough. Emotional abuse as a child can scar someone for the rest of their lives. Like adult victims, childhood emotional abuse victims can develop emotional and psychological problems such as depression, anxiety, distrust, self-doubt, lack of confidence, etc. They can also develop self-harm behaviors such as cutting themselves, eating disorders, substance abuse, and overall lack of self-care. Unlike adult victims, emotional abuse can affect childhood victims on a biological level that will not just last their entire lives but might even shorten them.

According to a 2013 study led by UCLA, emotional abuse and other toxic childhood stress can disrupt regulations of multiple bodily systems long-term, including the neuroendocrine and cardiovascular systems. This then puts the victim at a higher risk of diseases and an earlier death, especially if they don't have another loving parent to serve as a shield. [6]

That's why, if you notice any signs of a child being emotionally abused, you should not just sit back and let it happen. As I talked about earlier, the line between strict parenting and emotional abuse can be fairly hard to distinguish, and so it can be hard to tell when it's appropriate to intervene. Still, you can do some things to help ease the situation for the child.

Let's take the Grandma Jean example from earlier. Let's say that you're friends with Grandma Jean's daughter—her granddaughter's mother—and the two of them invite you to go clothes shopping with them and Grandma Jean's grand-daughter. While at the store, you all convince Grandma Jean's granddaughter to try on some sundresses.

"If she'll find any that fit," Grandma Jean re-marks.

You notice her granddaughter blush and shrink into herself before going into the dressing room, but you think nothing of it.

Dress after dress, the granddaughter comes out, and while you always think she looks nice, Grandma Jean keeps saying things like "It's too tight around the tummy" or "It's nice except for that problem area popping out under your arms."

While the granddaughter tries on the last dress, her mother confesses to you, while Grandma Jean isn't listening, that the granddaughter has been having a lot of stomach issues and high blood pressure since Grandma Jean came to live with them. You're worried, but you don't say anything.

When the granddaughter comes out in the final dress and says she really likes it, Grandma Jean says, "Are you sure? It really makes you look fat."

The granddaughter shrinks in on herself again, but her mother doesn't say anything. She almost seems to not notice anything is wrong.

Seeing the possible connection between Grandma Jean's comments and the granddaughter's growing health problems, you decide to not let it go and say to Grandma Jean, "Is that really appropriate to tell your granddaughter? She looks beautiful, tell her!"

Or maybe you decide not to confront Grandma Jean and instead turn to the granddaughter, smile, and say, "No, it doesn't. You look amazing. If you want it, you should buy it."

In this case, because the granddaughter's mother is there and is allowing this to happen, you might not feel that it is your place to say anything about the emotional abuse that appears to be occurring between Grandma Jean and her granddaughter. Yet it seems that the abuse is also affecting the granddaughter's health, if the stomach issues and high blood pressure that her mother mentioned aren't just a coincidence.

You won't always be able to directly stop or even report emotional child abuse or be there for them as overtly as you would be for a friend or family member going through a similar situation. Still, you can do what you can to negate the effects. Be their love shield whenever you can, whether that involves directly telling the abuser to stop or just countering their hurtful remarks.

In the next section, we are going to look at some steps you can take to recover from emotional abuse we have learned about so far. And if you like what you've learned so far, or you've found benefit, feel free to leave a review on Amazon. I really appreciate it as your feedback means a lot to me.

Part II: Recovering from Emotional Abuse

Chapter 7: Spotting Emotional Abuse Before It Takes Hold

The only way to make sure that you can get out of an abusive relationship is to realize that you are in one. This is often one of the hardest parts because emotional abuse can take on many different forms.

Even with all the information that I have provided, it can still be tricky to figure out whether or not you are being emotionally abused. If you are, it can still be just as easy to come up with excuses for your situation because the lines are often blurred.

We're going to take a look at a case study to help you see what emotional abuse looks like. If you notice that you identify with the situation and start to experience sadness, scared, or outrage for the people in the study, you might want to take a good look at the relationships you are in to see if you are excusing similar behaviors.

Margaret shared that had her abuser hit on their first date, she would have never gone another date with him, but what he actually did was much worse. After only nine months, they got married. She was emotionally vulnerable, and he helped her to feel secure.

At first, Margaret thought his jealousy was endearing. She thought it was cute that he cared so much. Then his behavior turned into little comments about her clothes, telling her that others would be staring at her skimpy outfits. Eventually, he would just tell her she dressed like a hooker.

They had a daughter, but he didn't really parent her. Margaret was forced to quit working so that she could care for their child. She was timed when she went to pick up their daughter from school. He would phone the house to make sure she got back in an appropriate timeframe.

Margaret stopped seeing her family and friends and only took care of her husband. The house would be clean when he came home. His shirts would be ironed for him, but Margaret said they would never be the shirts that he wanted.

Margaret started to get thrown off when her husband wouldn't let her go for regular check-ups. He would say that all she wanted to do was get naked in front of another man. Things went so far that she had to go to the emergency room and the doctors found that her ovaries had to be taken out. Her husband told her she had the operation done to spite him.

Margaret stayed in the relationship for seven years, and she believes, now, that had she stayed any longer, the relationship would have killed her. In the end, he did threaten to kill her.

It has been three years since she got out of the relationship and she is still going to therapy. By the time she got out, she believed that she was worthless and her identity had vanished. Before her relationship with him, she was an outgoing person.

Margaret's story of abuse showed many techniques that abusers will use. Her abuser liked to make her feel guilty. Margaret also displays many of the emotions and feelings that victims experience. Once Margaret noticed the effect the abuse was having on her and her child, she was able to get help.

Her husband often gaslighted her and made her believe that she couldn't do anything right. Margaret ended up relying on him, without realizing he was the cause of her feelings.

Emotionally abusive people will yell, bully, swear, threaten, mock, intimidate, and humiliate their victim. They will often become apologetic and charming, which keeps the victim around.

It's important to realize, though, that genuine temporary loss of control can actually happen, especially among those who live together for a long period of time. Life can become difficult, and nobody is impervious to frustration. If a partner or parent lashes out at you on a one-off occasion and you know this is unlike them, then you shouldn't misinterpret this as abuse, especially if they offer a genuine apology afterward. This type of thing could happen to anybody and is different from a cycle of abuse, which has a pattern and is systematic.

Am I Being Abused?

I have provided a brief quiz that you can take to see if you are in an emotionally abusive relationship. The sad thing is, sometimes it's harder to answer questions when the answers are staring us right in the face. This quiz works for romantic and non-romantic relationships. However, some questions are more likely to apply to romantic relationships than non-romantic ones, and you should be able to identify those when you come upon them. There is one caveat about the quiz; you have to be 100% honest with yourself.

- Do you find yourself fearing your partner?

    o   Yes, No, or Sometimes

- Do you find yourself avoiding certain topics because you are afraid you will anger them?

    o   Yes, No, or Sometimes

- Do you often feel like you can't do anything right?

    o   Yes, No, or Sometimes

- Do you feel that you deserve the mistreat-
  ment and hurt?

  - o   Yes, No, or Sometimes

- Do you ever wonder if you are crazy?

  - o   Yes, No, or Sometimes

- Do you ever feel helpless or emotionally
  numb?

  - o   Yes, No, or Sometimes

- Do they often yell at or humiliate you?

  - o   Yes, No, or Sometimes

- Do they often put you down or criticize
  you?

  - o   Yes, No, or Sometimes

- Do they make you embarrassed to be
  around friends and family?

  - o   Yes, No, or Sometimes

- Do they ignore or put down your accomplishments?

  o   Yes, No, or Sometimes

- Do they blame you for their actions?

  o   Yes, No, or Sometimes

- Do they view you as their property?

  o   Yes, No, or Sometimes

- Is their temper unpredictable?

  o   Yes, No, or Sometimes

- Have they ever threatened to hurt or kill you?

  o   Yes, No, or Sometimes

- Do they threaten to take your children?

  o   Yes, No, or Sometimes

- Have they ever threatened to kill themselves if you leave?

o   Yes, No, or Sometimes

- Do they make you have sex when you don't want to?

  o   Yes, No, or Sometimes

- Do they act possessive or jealous in order to limit who you get to see?

  o   Yes, No, or Sometimes

- Do they control the places you go and things you do?

  o   Yes, No, or Sometimes

- Do they isolate you from family and friends?

  o   Yes, No, or Sometimes

- Do they limit your access to transport and money?

  o   Yes, No, or Sometimes

- Do they constantly check up on you?

o   Yes, No, or Sometimes

The more questions you answer yes to, the more likely it is that you are in a relationship with an emotionally abusive person.

Recognizing Abuse in Hindsight

Sometimes, it can be hard to tell that you were in an abusive relationship when you were younger, especially if that relationship was with an adult you trusted as a child. Looking back, you'll probably be able to see that something wasn't quite right about it but might not be able to put your finger on it. Maybe you're repressing some of the worse parts or refusing to admit to yourself that the person was abusive.

No matter the reason for not seeing it before, it's important for you to know and acknowledge it now. Realizing you're currently in an abusive relationship can save you from an increasingly dangerous situation in the future; recognizing an abusive relationship in hindsight can help you begin to heal before you become self-destructive.

Now that you are an adult with some space and independence from your abuser, identifying abuse will be simultaneously easier and harder than when you are still in the abuser's grasp. It's easier in that they hopefully do not have as great of an influence over you as before and you can approach the situation with a clearer head. However, it's harder because, depending on how much time has passed and how much you are repressing, you might not remember enough to accurately assess what happened. Due to your grooming as a young abuse victim, you might be so biased as to not see things as badly as they were.

Still, it is possible to identify emotional abuse in your past. First, answer the same questions as above but thinking back on that particular relationship, whether it was with a past partner, a parent, grandparent, sibling, or someone else. Like before, some questions are more likely to apply to romantic than non-romantic relationships, and those questions will be obvious when you come to them. Also like before, the more questions you answer yes to, the more likely it is that this relationship was abusive.

It's important to remember, though, that these results can be tainted by personal bias. Not only could you be easier on your abuser because of remnants of your grooming, but there is other bad blood from that relationship, it could be making you recall things as worse than they really were. Key to telling the difference is checking your current self against the effects of emotional abuse. If you think you might have been emotionally abused as a child, that means also looking at the toxic behaviors that might surface in adulthood as a result of abuse.

You might require the help of a counselor or other mental health professional to identify and acknowledge past and present abuse. Nevertheless, once you do, you will then be able to take the first steps to dealing with your abuser and beginning the healing process.

Chapter 8: Dealing with Abusers

When you set boundaries in a relationship, it shows the victim how bad the abuse has gotten. When you can clearly see the abuser doesn't respect your boundaries constantly, the relationship might be on its last legs and the abuse becomes more obvious. Personal boundaries are rules that you tell your abuser can't be broken without creating consequences. Consequences are not punishments for breaking them; they are you doing what is right for you.

Boundaries for Any Relationship

Personal boundaries are what you have set for yourself for any relationship. These are some boundaries that you could put in place for yourself that you can carry with you:

- No abuse that is disguised as a joke

- No name calling either indirectly or directly where it could be overheard by others or myself

- No attempts to control by word or tone

- No implying that I am less valuable than any other just because my opinion is different

- No word games, no changing my words around to change their meanings

The consequences for violating any of these boundaries are as follows:

If somebody violated any boundary I have set and I feel safe telling them so, I will say, "I feel disrespected or threatened by your tone and words. I will leave so I can collect myself. I will come back later, and we can talk about them if you want to."

If I am verbally abused and I don't feel safe, I will act on the consequence and not try to explain it. I will leave until I feel safe to go back. If I don't feel safe in returning, I won't.

Leave the "You Make Me" and "You are" Out

You will see that the consequence for abuse doesn't have statements that start with "you are..." or "You make me feel..."

When you say "You are..." it defines and labels the person. Victims know how miserable and unfair it is to be labeled and it isn't fair to do it to anyone else. It doesn't matter how mean they have been to you.

When you say, "You make me feel...," you are giving them the power to hurt you. If you fall in this trap of thinking that somebody can change your feelings, you are allowing them to have the responsibility for your feelings. You are allowing the abuser to define who you are, and this could lead to low self-esteem.

Boundaries for Certain People

If you are being abused by a specific person, there are ways to set boundaries on them, too.

Here is an example: "When you interrupt me and squint your eyes, I feel disconnected and un-heard. I want you to see my point of view."

This is the consequence: "Since I can't control your thoughts and actions, I will leave and come back later to see if we can talk then."

Feeling Guilty for Setting Boundaries

When you first start setting boundaries, you might begin feeling guilty. You might feel like protecting yourself is a crime against them. The thought that you should do and be what they want is the source of guilt. After you have written a few boundaries, you might notice the guilt went away. While you were defining all the things that they said and did, you might realize that their actions are wrong. They should feel bad for how they be-haved, and you have the right to protect yourself from their actions and words.

Writing boundaries could help you see the abuse when it starts. When defining what you don't like, when you put it down on paper, you will learn to circumvent the abuse from the start instead of hanging around until you are a mess.

Writing down your boundaries gives you a sense of strength and responsibility that will diminish all the negativity that you once accepted willingly. You will stop seeing yourself as a victim and begin to see yourself as a person who can change your relationship and yourself.

Once you begin to enforce your boundaries, the abuse might increase. Your abuser might throw a temper tantrum like a child who has his toy taken away. They might not take your reactions well. You might need to split from this person but know if you do that, you can't go back to them no matter what.

Things Boundaries Can and Can't Do for a Relationship

The outcome of every relationship will be different. Everyone's feelings after they write down their boundaries will be different, too. Writing boundaries will help you to see many things but some might not come to pass, like:

- You might think your abuser will change their ways when their words and actions were brought to his attention. They might just get meaner and angrier that you aren't taking responsibility anymore.

- You might think you can improve the relationship since you know how to behave the right way. They might not want to behave in different ways.

There are two feelings that can help you get rid of your victim mentality:

- A sense of empowerment you might develop after realizing you don't need to feel guilty for having good mental health.

- Being disgusted that all the abuse happened in what you once thought was a loving relationship.

Responding to Verbal Abuse

If you have been dealing with verbal abuse in your relationship, you have to learn certain responses to say to your abuser. When you can understand why specific responses are effective, you will be able to enforce your limits better.

You are establishing boundaries when you set limits. These boundaries will protect your integrity. They define you. All verbal abuse will violate boundaries in one way or another. If you have been verbally abused, you have to respond in a way that shows you are aware of the violation. When you respond the right way, it confirms or reestablishes your boundaries and enforces your limits. Here are some examples of how verbal abuse will violate your boundaries:

1. If your significant other totally ignores you, if they look through you like you weren't there at all, this is a violation of your boundaries. They are treating you just like your individuality doesn't even exist. Like you don't have anything to set you apart from the scenery. We normally don't

think about ourselves as needing boundaries, but we need to. When a person violates our boundaries, it is a form of abuse.

2. If they call you names, they are violating
   your boundaries. The abuser is defining
   you on their terms instead of yours. They
   are treating you like your boundaries that
   define and establish your individuality
   don't exist.

3. If your significant other orders you to do
   something, they are violating your boundaries. Can you see how this violates boundaries? When someone orders you to do
   something, they are treating you like you
   aren't an individual to be asked or con-
   sulted. They are treating you like you don't
   have any boundaries, nothing that sepa-
   rates you and the abuser, like you are an
   extension of them like you are an instru-
   ment to be used at their will. This is a horrible invasion of boundaries.

4. Another violation of boundaries is denial.
   If your abuser discounts or denies you,
   then they have violated your boundaries.

They are acting as if they have access to your mind and know what you have gone through. According to them, it was all in your imagination. It didn't happen. They might say something like: "You don't know what you are talking about."

These show how important it is to respond to verbal abuse in ways that will reconfirm and reestablish boundaries.

Verbal abuse is not a conflict, it is a violation. There is a huge difference between abuse and conflict. With conflicts, every person wants something different. To be able to resolve the conflict, they will discuss their reasons, needs, and wants while trying to find a solution. A solution might not be found, but neither one controls, dominates, or forces the other one.

Verbal abuse is a lot different from conflicts. If we give verbal abuse a definition from a boundary violation standpoint, it would get described as a disregard of, an intrusion on, a person by another individual who disregards boundaries in a pursuit of dominance, superiority, and power over by overt or covert ways.

If you have been verbally abused, you need to take some time to evaluate your relationship before you respond. Is there any possibility for improvement? Here are some questions that might help you evaluate your relationship:

- Do they show you good will?

- Do they make your life richer?

- Do they think like you or share your dreams?

- Do you feel an actual connection to them?

- Do they bring joy into your life?

Having goodwill in a relationship means it brings warmth and honesty that comes from the deepest sense of truth. It is being concerned with another person's wellbeing along with a desire to understand each other. It can be shown by psychologically moving toward one another while trying to reach mutual respect and understanding.

Even though you might experience verbal abuse, if your partner shows good will toward you and you answer "yes" to the questions above, there might be a chance they will change once you decide to enforce your boundaries.

If the relationship is new and you notice signs of verbal abuse, it would be wise to get out of the relationship now before it's too late. Any person who feels the need to have a scapegoat, control, and dominate isn't going to easily change if they do at all. This is very true in a brand-new relationship where they feel they haven't invested a lot of energy or time. Once the newness of the relationship wears off, they will probably get more abusive. If they are just trying to see how much you are going to take, they might change fast if they realize you aren't going to tolerate the behavior.

If you have been in the relationship for a long time and are dealing with verbal abuse, if it is important to you, and if you have decided to respond to the abuse, you will soon realize if your partner is going to stop their behavior. You are going to get some self-esteem and awareness out of it.

Responses are designed to create an impact that will stop your abuser, protect you from more abuse, and enforces your boundaries. These responses might allow the abuser to see what they have been doing, understand they can't continue to do it, and stop abusing.

You might have discovered from the abuse that trying to understand and explain hasn't improved the relationship at all. You need to respond in a different way; a way that makes an intellectual, psychological, and emotional impact of your partner.

They might change when they realize you understand you are being abused, you have set boundaries, you aren't going to take their behavior anymore, and you mean what you are saying, even if they repeatedly say: "You don't know what you are talking about."

Never, ever blame yourself if they don't change. If they aren't willing to make a difference or change, it is time to get out of the relationship.

Here are some suggestions on how to start the process:

- Tell them that you aren't going to respond like you used to.

- If it will be easier for you, write them a letter. I know I have a hard time talking to my ex face-to-face.

- Tell them that you aren't happy with what you have put up with from him.

- Let them know you want a great relationship with them.

- You want to see changes in the way they communicate with you.

- You have tried to explain to them about what is bothering you about their behavior, but you don't feel like they have listened.

- Let them know that you are telling them what you do and don't want out of the relationship.

- Tell them you have boundaries and you will tell them that you will call them out if they cross the line.

- Ask for their cooperation.

They might not realize any changes are necessary. This is because they aren't the ones suffering the abuse. They might say something like, "You are trying to ruin this relationship" or "You are causing problems." If they do, you respond with: "You need to stop this right now! No more accusations!"

They might seem blind to the fact or deny they are being abusive. You might still impact them with your response. The response is designed to wake up your abuser and show them that their behavior is unacceptable and inappropriate to you. There are some people who will change their behavior when they begin to get responses from you. Other people are completely resistant to change.

If your significant other stays abusive, it isn't your fault, and it isn't your responsibility. When you take these steps, you know you will be able to see the verbal abuse when it happens and you will be able to respond in the right way.

If they catch you off guard with the verbal abuse, if you get stunned, too confused, in pain, shocked, or confused to respond immediately to the abuse, you have been in a toxic relationship for way too long. You need to get help now.

In order to respond from a place of strength, you have to know that verbal abuse might be signs that they are emotionally immature. People might respond with temper tantrums or calling the other nasty names just like a child would. When a person gets called names, it makes them wonder: "What did I do that makes them think this way of me?"

A child calling another child a name and an adult calling another adult a bad name are on the same level of emotional maturity. Children haven't reached mental maturity to know better so their name calling doesn't bother us. Adults who still like calling other people names could be dangerous.

Another example of immaturity is countering. If you have been around children who are trying to learn the right way to do things, you might have heard one of them say: "You don't do it that way." "You are wrong."

To four-year-olds, their view is the only one. A child wants the world to be fixed in a certain way. Mature adults know that it isn't and there are many people and many points of view.

While we mature, we learn to respect other people's perspectives and views. We also learned ways to appropriately express our anger. We mimic our parents when dealing with anger. Parents can unknowingly or knowingly teach by example. By the time we get to be adults, we should have learned to express anger the right way. A person who is an abuser missed this learning. This is why they are abusive and angry.

When anger is expressed the right way, it will never be blaming, destructive, abusive, or accusatory. If anger does get expressed abusively, it will be hurtful and destructive. You can express anger in healthy ways. If a person responds to abuse forcefully by saying: "Stop that!" they are using anger to protect themselves. Using anger constructively is a lot different from destructive accusations and blames.

- Blame: "You know what you did!"

- Accusation: "You are trying to get out of it!"

These are both forms of abusive anger. You can imagine how confusing this abuse could be to a person who has heard it their entire life.

BE CAREFUL: If you feel shocked, stunned, or are in too much pain to talk, if your partner seems to be angry and out of control, if you are afraid of him, if he has threatened you, hurt you, or hit you, you don't need to deal with this behavior alone. You have to question how healthy it would be if you stayed around them.

When you respond to verbal abuse, you have to respond with strength so you can make an impact. It isn't going to be easy, so take it slow. You aren't dealing with word games when you live with abuse. You are fighting for your soul, sanity, and spirit.

If you get caught off guard, it might be hard to think about what to say. It is easy to stay calm around a stranger who is abusive like a driver who blows past you and cuts you off in traffic, then staying calm with an abusive partner. This happens for many reasons. The main one is that your heart is open to your partner and they have the power to reject you. Abuse is basically rejection. It is toxic and painful.

BE CAREFUL: Don't ever deceive yourself that you have to stay calm when you are being treated unfairly. You keep your serenity because you know that you have the right to a nurturing environment and to protect your boundaries.

When Responding to Verbal Abuse

- Be aware. Think hard about the present. Be aware of what your senses are telling you. What do you see? How do they sound to you? What are you feeling?

- Realize when you are being yelled at, ordered around, and being put down. These are all signs of abuse. Abuse is destructive, disabling, and unjust.

- Respond with firmness and authority that tells your abuser you mean business. Let them know you are serious and you won't tolerate any more abuse.

- Understand your abuser isn't speaking in an adult, rational way.

- Put distance between you and your abuser by noticing the immaturity for what it really is.

- Understand you are responding to someone who is trying to establish superiority, dominate, or control you.

- Understand that it isn't healthy to remain in an abusive relationship.

- Understand that you haven't done anything to cause them to abuse you.

Once you decide to respond to abuse, you have to speak clearly and firmly, stand up tall and straight, look your abuser in the eye, take a deep breath, hold your head up, and let your stomach expand with the air intake.

Being able to respond and recognize verbal abuse will take dedication, determination, effort, energy, and time. Even if your partner stops abusing you, there will still be some things in the relationship that might have to be worked on. If they are willing to work on it with you, if he can acknowledge his behavior, if he is willing to change, if he has good will toward you, if he asks you what you need and want out of the relationship, you both might be able to build a better relationship.

How quickly will you see results and no more abuse? A lot of it depends on your partner. There is no way you can "make it happen" by yourself. If they won't or can't stop screaming at you, even if you have told them to "Stop!" and if they continue to think you caused their anger, you shouldn't expect results. If they don't want to change, then they aren't. You are going to know in about a month if they are willing to change. They will have either continue to abuse you or they have stopped abusing you.

If they care about you and if they truly want a relationship with you, you might see results within one week.

Some responses to every category of abuse are below. You don't have to memorize all the responses. You could be able to get the message across in your own words.

Responses to Abuse

If you are in a very difficult situation and need a fast response that will work for any verbal abuse, you can use: "Stop talking like that right now!"

- Withholding

This is silent treatment. You don't have to sit through endless hours of silence that get interrupted by your expression of interest, comment on a news story, or occasional question while you constantly get a response from your partner. It doesn't matter if you are at the beach, shopping, watching television, at home, or out to dinner. If you have sat through hours or even days of silence, get up and walk away from wherever you are and say: "I am extremely bored with you right now."

Leave and stay away for as long as you would like. You might or might not make an impact, but you won't be bored anymore. Reading, going for ice cream, or going for a walk is less painful and not as boring as sitting around hoping for a response and getting nothing but the "silent treatment."

A friend had enough of this type of behavior and decided to put in her earphones and listened to her favorite music when she sat down to dinner with her partner. She hummed and gestured all through dinner to the music she was listening to. Her strange behavior had an impact on her partner. He was soon gesturing trying to get her to talk to him.

- Countering

If your partner misconstrues what you said or counters your perceptions, feelings, and ideas, you could say decisively, "Stop!" while holding your arms up and straight out in front of you with your palm facing your partner. Follow "Stop" with: "Please listen to what I am saying." Repeat your original statement while speaking distinctly and slowly.

Never try to explain what you meant or said since they will only counter the explanation. Repeat this every time they counter you. You have the right to your own perceptions and thoughts. If you remain alert and aware and stop the countering every time, you might have an effect on your partner's behavior to the point that he actually stops countering.

If you express your feelings about something he has said and he responds: "I don't see it that way," that's fine. He isn't countering you. He is just stating he has a different view.

If your partner states an opinion to you, you repeat it back to them verbatim to show them you understood what they said, and they counter your repeat statement, stop immediately. Never try to express you understand his second statement. Realize you have an increased awareness and trust that you understood their original statement. They are countering you. They don't want to understand anything with you. When you realize this, just say, "Hold on! I can't follow you.

Would you please write it down so I can see what you are saying?" or "Cut it out!" or "Stop countering me!"

If they refuse, don't spend any more time trying to figure them out, and never take anything they say seriously. They aren't trying to understand you or get you to understand them. If you try to understand their meaning, you will only get frustrated and confused.

Another response that works for most situations is: "So you say," say this very empathically, slowly, and calmly. This leaves it at being undebatable while leaving the abuser with complete responsibility for their statement while leaving you with your opinion.

There might be times your abuser wants to make it a challenge. After you have expressed an opinion like "I thought the movie was great" and they come back with "You can't prove that," the only way to respond is a simple, "No." You have to disengage at this point. Leave the room, go for a walk, take yourself out to eat, take the dog to the park, or visit a friend.

You have a right to your own perspective, opinion, and view. There might be the same number of views about something as there are people on the planet. Everybody's view will fit into their beliefs, experience, and perspective. When you get told that your views are wrong, it feels like somebody has taken over your mind and body and annihilated your experience.

- Discounting

This is a troublesome form of abuse. How can you respond to it? It seems like the damage has been done. You have been hurt and put down by a jab. When you try to protect with "Why did you say that?" or "That isn't the truth," or "That wasn't nice, you made me feel bad," you are being told that what you experienced didn't count. It has been discounted with "You are jumping to conclusions!" or "You always blow everything out of proportion." This is a horrible invasion of boundaries. The abuser is trying to take over your mind and is trying to replace your ideas with his.

Never try to understand how they can say or think those things. Don't try to get them to understand that you aren't jumping to conclusions or you aren't blowing things out of proportion. Don't try to protest by saying: "Why did you say that?" Respond with outrage.

What will make them listen? Try: "Cut it out!" "Hold on! I don't want to hear you talk that ever again!" "Stop that talk right now!"

These responses might get opposed by your abuser. They can't be discounted easily. When you experience verbal abuse and get caught by surprise, use them.

If you are more confused than outraged when you hear things like "You don't know what you are talking about!", respond forcefully like you have made a huge discovery and throw your hands up while stating "Ha! That's what you believe!" This works wonders with "you" statements. If they say, "yes," just say with mystery and meaning, "I see."

The main thing your abuser will avoid is taking responsibility for the things he says. That response will let them know that you are holding them responsible and that you know the beliefs are theirs and not yours.

- Abuse Disguised as a Joke

When you get put down and you tell your abuser that you don't like what they said to you, they respond with "It was only a joke." They might laugh loudly about it. This is abuse that is being disguised as a joke. To be able to respond to this type of abuse, you have to know that they are putting you down to make them look better.

There are cases when a person tells another that they didn't like what the abuser said to them, the abuser takes this as an attack and instead of apologizing, the abuser puts them down again by telling them they don't have a sense of humor.

If you constantly hear this from your partner, know that they are violating your boundaries and are trying to define your most intimate quality, your sense of humor. Don't try to explain why it wasn't funny. Don't try to tell them the types of jokes you think are funny. Don't try to explain to them the types of jokes that you don't find funny and you don't want them said to you. Don't ask them to explain what they meant. Don't waste time wondering if they even understood how it sounded especially if they act like it was funny to them. Wonder about their maturity level.

Any time you get ridiculed, denigrated, disparaged, or put down, or you don't like what you are hearing, try to respond with "I am wondering after you have said (the put down) (laughed at me) (interrupted me), does that make you feel important? I want you to think about it."

Leave the room. Tell them you need some time alone. You are going to make a huge impact on them if you take this approach. Don't talk to them. If they try to engage you in conversation, you could respond with "I'll get back to you later" or "I don't want to talk about it."

• Diverting and Blocking

Be aware of your feeling. If you are feeling frustrated when you ask your partner about something that concerns you or when you tell them about something that is important to you, you are experiencing diverting and blocking.

Because you have the right to manage your own affairs, if your partner is diverting and blocking you from getting any information you need, they are violating your boundaries. You are being treated like you don't have rights.

If you ask a question and it gets diverted or blocked, don't respond to statements that are getting thrown like roadblocks, and don't respond to statements that divert you from your purpose. Tell your abuser to "look at me!" and repeat that question. For example:

"Where did the money go?"

"Are you telling me that I have to sort through all this when you can't balance your checkbook?"

"Look at me! What did you do with the $5,000?"

"If you don't like the way I handle the money, then you can worry about the finances."

"Look at me! Where did the $5,000 go?"

Keep repeating the question until they respond. Remain focused on your feelings. If might be easy to have a desire to defend yourself, but you might become diverted. Their response could be either a statement saying they aren't going to answer you or an answer to your question.

You could also say, "Stop diverting me."

Blame and Accusation

You have to respond with awareness to blame and accusations if you want to live abuse-free. Being aware of blame and accusations and knowing that blame and accusations are violations of boundaries gives you the freedom to leave your partner if they don't stop.

You might want to stay in the relationship because you think you can explain to your abuser that what they are blaming you for or accusing you of isn't true. You want them to understand you and realize you aren't an enemy.

When someone snaps or yells at you, tells you that you aren't acting right, acting dumb, smart, trying to pick a fight, interrupting, getting in the last word, or imagining things, they are abusing you. You can respond with: "Stop blaming or accusing me right now! Stop it!"

You can also choose any of these:

- "I think you know better than that!"

- "I don't want to ever hear you say that again!"

- "Don't ever talk to me like that."

- "Remember who you are talking to!"

Don't waste time trying to explain to them that you weren't doing what they are accusing you of doing. Just tell them to stop it. Your abuser makes up a story about your motives and then tells them to you. Nobody has the right to do that to you.

If you are being abused and feel like you can explain things that he will understand, remember: If somebody began throwing rocks at your house, you will easily tell them to stop than try to explain to them why they shouldn't throw them. Verbal abuse is like a rock getting thrown at your house.

Criticizing and Judging

These are lies about a person's performance and qualities. They will hurt your self-esteem. When you hear criticism and judgments, you should ask yourself who has the authority to judge me? No one but me.

Nobody has the right to criticize and judge your performance and qualities. Defining violates boundaries. Presuming is an invasion. If you want to respond to criticizing and judging, you have to speak authoritatively, emphatically, firmly, and strongly. Let your anger support you:

- "This doesn't concern you!"

- "Do you hear what you just said?"

- "Mind your own business."

- "Stop judging me!"

- "Keep your comments to yourself."

- "Stop criticizing me."

- "That is complete nonsense."

- "Enough of that."

- "I won't accept that kind of talk."

Leave the area if possible, don't continue with the discussion. Any more discussion will dilute your response.

Name Calling

This is an invasion of your boundaries. Name calling is very abusive; it needs to be responded to with outrage.

- "I don't want to hear you call anyone else a name in this house."

- "Stop that! Don't ever call me names again."

If someone calls you names, you have to realize that nobody has a right to call you names. There is no justification for calling anyone names. If you have gotten used to being called names, you have to understand that you can live a life that is free from this type of abuse. There is a possibility that the abuser doesn't have the capacity to love anyone in a healthy relationship.

Ordering

If your partner orders you around, they have forgotten that you are a person who has the right to pursue happiness, liberty, and life. You are free, and if they want something from you, they have to ask nicely and courteously. You can remind them of your boundaries and tell them, "Who do you think you are giving orders to?", "Do you hear yourself?" or "I don't take orders from anybody." "Could you ask nicely, please?"

If they give you orders starting with "we" like "We are leaving now," you can remind them of the boundaries by stating, "That isn't what I had in mind."

Threatening

If you are threatened with sexual or physical harm or think a situation feels like it might get threatening, it is important that you find help as quickly as you can.

If you get verbally threatened in different ways, your partner is trying to manipulate you. If you don't understand what it is they want, they are threatening to leave, or they stay out all night, you can tell them "no" when they ask you for something in the future. Being threatened with a pending disaster will shatter your serenity and your boundaries.

Respond calmly and clearly as you can with "Don't bother me with threats, please," "Stop with the threats," "Leave me alone," or "I don't want to hear it."

Abusive Anger

While reading through this book, if you have caught yourself feeling or thinking that you are too afraid to respond as we have suggested, you might be in a relationship with a person who is addicted to anger. You have to respect yourself and your fear and follow that cautions in this chapter.

Abusive anger is verbal abuse and is linked to needing to "blow up," control, put someone down, get one up on someone, and dominate.

How can you respond to abusive anger? People I have spoken to who had lived through abusive anger all felt afraid with this type of anger.

A good rule of thumb for dealing with a person who is extremely angry is to stay away. If you are being yelled or snapped at, you might need to put some strategies in place that might have an impact on your abuser. These might motivate them to change or give you time to leave the relationship if need be.

If your abuser begins to snap or yell at you, you might feel too scared or stunned to respond. You might be able to get put some distance between yourself and them by thinking of them not as a partner, champion, friend, children, or parent but as an argumentative, recalcitrant, tantrum-throwing, screaming, or petulant child. If you can visualize one of these the next time they yell at you, you could respond with "You will not raise your voice to me" or "I don't like that tone of voice." You might even be fast enough to say, "Stop! Take a breath and try to speak nicely to me."

An angry person might abuse you more if you have friends around just to make you feel bad. During this situation, if you speak up, you might seem "out of line" or "making things up." Try to respond with "Even though nobody here knows anything about this, I am very disappointed with you."

Many people find it hard to respond to abusive anger. This anger is unexpected and expressed with words that catch you by surprise. Your mind will begin to try to understand, analyze, or search for what they are yelling about and what it means in relation to you.

The key when responding to abusive anger is to not pay attention to their words. When you get yelled or snapped at, they are abusing you. You don't have to take it, understand it, or analyze it.

You might find it hard to respond to abusive anger. Stay alert and watch for signs of anger. The moment you hear an angry tone, respond with: "Hold on!" and then leave. If you are speaking with them on the phone, just hang up. When you see their jaw begin to clench, face turning red, rigid body, you can respond with "Hold on!" or leave. If you sense any type of tension, leave.

The responses might help you make an impact and stay away from abuse. If you can learn to be aware of the angry attack when it begins, you might be able to stop it or leave immediately, you could break the pattern of getting caught by their words. If you stop trying to understand what they are talking about, you will be able to respond faster and with clarity.

You can't change anybody. If your partner is abusive and doesn't want to change, you might have to confront the reality that you can't have a healthy life in a toxic environment. You don't have to live your life constantly on guard, always being prepared for abuse.

Try to solve the problem before it begins. The easiest way to stay away from abuse is to spot an abuser and stay away from the relationship before it happens.

If you are looking to start a new relationship, be picky. See the difference between the things you want and what you are getting. See if your new partner shares the same reality.

Use these questions as an evaluation. You have to trust your own feelings when answering these questions. If you come up with just one answer you don't like, there's a good chance you won't have a good relationship:

- Do they assume based on unreliable evidence?

- Is there joy in their life?

- Do they remember or understand things differently from reality?

- Do you like his ideas? Do you feel comfortable around him?

- Does their world house bad guys and good guys?

- Do you find yourself understanding the same meanings, laughing with them, and connecting with them?

- When you spend time with them, is it pleasant?

- Do you feel a friendly quality in the relationship?

- Do they argue against your experiences, feelings, ideas, and thoughts?

- Do they make you feel relaxed?

- Do other people think he is distrustful?

- Can you actually be yourself without being criticized?

- Do they use humor to hurt other people? Is their humor uncomfortable, intimidating, or bitter?

- Do they share their interests with you and are they interested in yours?

- Do they exude understanding and warmth?

- Do they speak honestly and openly about themselves?

It doesn't matter if you are, never have been, or were in an abusive relationship. The above questions give you some criteria that you can use to evaluate any new or old relationships. What is more important are your own feelings. If you have the slightest feeling that something isn't right, it isn't.

Chapter 9: Avoid and Remove Abusers

An emotionally abusive relationship makes your life completely miserable and it can damage your self-confidence. The only advice I can give you is to get out. Being in a relationship that makes you feel horrible, worthless, and completely useless isn't healthy but it the fastest way to destroy your self-confidence.

Getting out of an abusive relationship might seem hard, especially if the abuser has succeeded in convincing you that nobody else is going to want you. They have criticized you so much that your self-confidence is completely gone. They do this to keep you trapped. The first thing you need to do is to rebuild your self-confidence to be able to leave the abusive relationship.

The second thing to do is to rebuild your social life. Many abusers keep their victims isolated. They won't let them see their friends. This usually happens because the abuser feels jealous or they are just sadistic. Some abusers enjoy watching their victims suffer knowing they don't have any-one they can turn to. Rebuilding friendships al-lows you to move away from your abuser and learn how to understand your emotions. This will help you make better decisions for your life.

The next step is becoming financially independ-ent. An abuser will usually control the money to keep the victim from leaving them. Having a job and your own money gives you the power to leave the relationship. Even if you don't decide to leave, having money and a job can give you leverage with the abuser. It gives you the power to tell them: "I have my own money and a job. If you continue to act this way, I will leave." Most of them aren't emotionless creatures. If they weren't scared of you leaving, they wouldn't keep you un-der lock and key.

A word of warning for becoming financially inde-pendent: if you don't already have a job, be care-ful when you first start looking for one. Your abuser will know the possibilities of you getting a job and becoming financially independent, so they might try to foil your attempts. Don't apply for any jobs from the home computer or even your own laptop. Use a friend's, family member's, or a library's computer instead. Same with where you store resume (although you can't keep that on something public like a library computer). If you access either an application or your resume from a computer that your abuser has access to, they could sabotage it. Also make sure to give the recruiters your cellphone number, not a number you share with your abuser, and keep your cellphone on you at all times. They will do whatever they can to maintain control over you.

Why Do Some People Control Others?

You need to continue to ask, "Is it them or me?" You constantly feel anxious around them; you believe that you can make things better. You want to feel the same love you felt when the relationship began. Your biggest fear is that what they think of you is actually true. You aren't lovable.

The bad news is that you have let yourself get caught up in their web. However, there is good news. You can get out of it if you really want to. You have to understand what control is about.

There are many reasons why a person wants to control another. Here is a look at their behavior:

- They project their fears of being unlovable and inadequate on you.

- They are full of powerlessness and help-lessness.

- They want to make sure you won't reject or abandon them.

- They use people to make themselves feel better.

- They project their anxiety onto others so that they don't have to deal with it.

Some people seek control for one of these reasons, and for others, it's a combination of them. As I discussed earlier, people who are abused could go on to pass this abuse onto others, including their own children. Because they are now emotionally insecure and have lost control, they might look to take control of others. It might make them feel as though they've regained some sense of control in their own lives, or maybe they are suffering from the "misery loves company" mentality. No matter what the reason, they are now making others—spouses, partners, children, dependent parents or siblings—feel what they felt. Not all abusers have been abused, and not everyone who has been abused will become abusive, but it's always a possibility.

In some cases—like with psychopathic and malignant narcissistic abuse—the abuser might just get a sadistic joy out of controlling others. Those are very extreme and frightening situations, but fortunately, they are not very common.

Just remember, your abuser's controlling behavior isn't about you, ever.

Take Control

There are ways you can get out from under their control:

- Take back power

The fastest way to take back your power is to walk away if you have to. This will let you move forward from a place of power instead of fear.

- Set limits to their emotional outbursts and criticism

Let them know that you will listen to any concerns they might have about your actions and the way they might impact them. They have to understand that you aren't going to listen to them if all they are going to do is attack you.

- Think about their concerns

What things will you do for them? What won't you ever do for them? Be sure you keep these requests in line with your integrity and well-being. Never agree to do things just to try to save the relationship or to keep the peace, especially if you know deep down that it isn't right.

- Find experiences and people that will celebrate you

Find a way to reconnect with the most powerful person you know: yourself. That person will never allow someone to treat them in this manner. Connect and engage with others that love and support you for who you are.

- Be honest and clear with yourself and your partner

Think about your needs, goals, and values. Be sure each decision is in line with your needs and highest self. Let them know what you are willing to and what you won't do for them. It doesn't matter what you do, don't let them intimidate you. Use a powerful "NO" and be clear that he either accept the "NO" or the two of you will go separate ways.

Ten Ways to Know if You are Ready to Leave the Abuser

Leaving an abuser will be the hardest thing you ever do. It will make you feel unsure. You are going to doubt yourself. The following is to help people who have found themselves in this situation to see the signs that they are ready to leave. This will help them feel strong enough to walk away.

1. You decide to take care of yourself.

Your friend might have asked you, "Why did you stop wearing mascara?"

I hadn't realized that everyone else had noticed I had stopped wearing makeup. I had worn mascara since my mom introduced me to it in my early teens. When I wore mascara, my boyfriend at the time would have a fit. I decided to stop wearing it.

I went to therapists to help rebuild my personal life. With time, the panic attacks stopped. I woke up one day and decided to begin taking care of myself again and the first step was to lose some weight I had put on due to stress eating.

I slowly took back my life, and it shone back at me. I stopped wearing lounge pants and tee shirts and began wearing slacks, skirts, dresses, perfume, makeup, and painted my lashes with mascara. Once I reclaimed my beauty, I didn't care what he did or said to try to put me down.

Don't underestimate how powerful self-love is and how powerful feeling beautiful can be. Each harmful word the abuser says to you to try to break your spirit will boomerang back to them since you are beautiful and strong both outside and in.

2. You don't see them in your future.

With time, I had made numerous compromises and I knew deep down that I could never marry him, own a home with him, or have children with him. I began to tell people those things didn't interest me, hoping to convince myself in the process. About three months before I decided to move out, my future vision changed. I saw a stable, loving relationship and a house. I didn't see him in these plans, and this gave me peace. It showed me that I could have a life without him in it.

Listen to your dreams and hopes. Breathe life into them and fill them with your energy. Take notice when the abuser begins to be in them less and less. This took my self-confidence to a new level. I could finally confront what he had really been doing to me.

3. You see that your abuser chooses not to help themselves.

I thought for a long time that he was helpless and couldn't do anything for himself and I never thought of his behavior as abusive.

Just like most, I would tell myself, "I won't ever stay with anyone who abuses me." The truth was once I realized I was in that situation, I didn't leave since I thought because I loved him that love could conquer all, just like he promised. I wouldn't leave since I thought he has been hurt. I didn't leave since we had professed our love for each other. I had been beaten by years of guilt trips and abuse, so I thought I didn't deserve better.

It took a long time to get past all the smoke screens and break the mirrors that he had put up. He had been deflecting the real problem. When I finally saw my life without him, I could see the truth. I wasn't abused because he was raised by toxic parents, because he used to have a drug problem, or because of his past. I was abused because it thrilled him. This gave me the power to leave him more than anything else ever had.

Here's a hard truth you might have to face: if they keep promising to get help but never make any progress, they're probably never going to change. If they had meant it, they would've started the process already. If they've started but keep relapsing into their abusive behavior, it means the same thing. They have chosen not to help themselves, and you have to start putting yourself first.

4. You give priority to your health rather than the abuser.

Disengagement from the abuser happens when the victim begins to change from just thoughts to taking action. You may have started putting money aside to be ready to leave. You may be asserting yourself more and setting boundaries that you normally wouldn't have made. When you find yourself in an argument, you might say, "I don't like being treated like this, stop, please."

Most women will begin to take the advice of putting the abuse on record. I remember shaking violently when I would go to the local women's abuse shelter to talk to counselors and to see my doctor. I would feel guilty for taking these steps, but I was constantly taking steps to be independent.

You need to constantly remind yourself that you have to keep yourself safe. It isn't your responsibility to try and protect the abuser. It would be a good idea to talk with a lawyer to get help to end a marriage, get custody of a child, or divide up the property.

5. You no longer pretend everything is fine.

I had a lunch date with some friends and every one of them asked me, "How are things going with your significant other?"

I had to muster up some courage to tell them that he was abusing me and I was trying to leave him. None of them judged me. Surprisingly, they offered emotional support, helpful numbers, and spare beds.

This showed me that even though I was in a difficult situation, I shouldn't blame myself. People truly felt sorry for me. I had to stop being secretive about it. Within a week, I was gone.

6. You don't like spending time with them.

I stopped going to his drug dealer's house. I stopped going to bars with him. I stopped spending time with his friends. When I was near him, I literally got sick to my stomach. I felt covered in sludge. After each encounter, I would shower and scrub myself until I felt clean. I was trying to get rid of any trace of him. I began to reconnect with friends and started spending time with nice people who were genuinely kind.

7. You get drastic and "cause" the breakup.

It is hard to do the breaking up and most victims will try to force the abuser to do it. Narcissistic abusers want things on their terms. They would rather throw you to the side than to deal with being humiliated by you breaking up with him. Most abusers will even lie about the breakup to their friends to make themselves look better. You will be in the most danger right before and right after you leave the abuser. You have to be careful of how you try to trigger the breakup since the abuser might be vengeful. You have to ALWAYS have an escape plan in place that will keep you safe.

8. Stop letting the abuser take credit.

My ex started taking credit for my achievements. If I was on the news for my writing or quoted in media, it was because he was the one who designed my website. It never had anything to do with me pitching the ideas to clients and doing the work that had to be done. He constantly lied to everyone, telling them he paid for my education along with everything else.

Near the time I left, I began calling him out when I heard him try to claim credit for my next achievement. I wasn't going to live in his fantasy world anymore, and I didn't care if what I achieved hurt him. I learned to put myself first. There wasn't one insult that could break me.

9. Your male friends came back.

If I spoke to a male friend or colleague or if a male stranger smiled at me, I would be in trouble. I also had the ability to turn gay men straight. He would stare at me if I even spoke to a mutual male friend. It just got easier to stay away from men.

Even after all his stories about being cheated on, I knew he was controlling me and it was an unhealthy relationship. I quit putting all his weaknesses above myself. I began to reference my internal model, my parents, to remember what a healthy relationship is all about. You can have friends of both sexes and trust one another totally.

If you like hanging with platonic male friends, it is another sign that you are ready to get back to the real world. If you find yourself starting to get crushes on some friends and think about having a relationship without your toxic partner, this is your gut telling you that you can have better people in your life instead of your toxic, abusive partner. Your mind is getting you ready for the next chapter in your life.

10. You know the breakup drama will be worth the life after.

"I will pack my things and go back home," I bravely told my therapist. My ex was the person who sponsored my visa and he used it often to threaten my immigration status. While I was simply moving from the UK to pursue my dreams, it was a big deal when he threatened this. I had the mindset that starting over was better than telling my friends and family the truth. I had messed up badly and chosen a very bad man. What would my colleagues think if they knew? The thoughts tore me in half.

Think about leaving as being offered two choices. One choice is staying in the same life. The other is you will wake up away from your abusive partner, past all the pain and complications. Some people will choose to stay in the relationship while others will choose the second choice and realize that they aren't staying in the relationship due to love. They are only staying because they fear the breakup.

Think about that and remind yourself that our brains love to amplify anxiety. The drama of a breakup is ugly but if you take the time to work through it, you will realize that you can make a plan. You see that it is quite doable.

The abuser will see you getting your strength back and putting distance between the two of you. It will upset them, and the abuse might get worse for a while. They will try to make you pay for trying to shine and having the guts to stand up for yourself. While you stand firm in knowing who you are and being rooted in self-respect, you will start to become stubborn. Fight for this stubbornness. Fight for the future. It will be the best decision you ever make.

Leaving

You have finally decided to leave an abusive relationship. Your partner might have been too abusive or they chose not to respect your boundaries. They may have crossed too many lines when you confronted them about the abuse.

Remember, when you leave an abuser, this will be the most dangerous time for you. Don't be scared.

First off, know that what you are about to do is the hardest decision you have made in your life. It is going to take loss, pain, and time for you to get where you are today. Getting yourself out of the abuser's web is difficult and tricky. If there are children involved, it could make the situation harder, but you can still do it.

Second, understand that your physical and emotional safety needs to be your priority. The goal of this chapter is to give you a guide to help you get out of the abusive situation safely. It can be a bit daunting, but you've made it to this point.

You have been on a weird journey. You have learned some misconceptions about emotional abuse. You have learned the signs to look for to know if you are in an abusive relationship. If you have a friend that you are worried about, then you know what to do for them. Don't cut them out of your life if they can't leave their partner when you want them to.

Maybe you have realized that you are the one who is abusing others. Hopefully, when you learned that bit of information, you went to a therapist to get help for your issues. You have to be honest and upfront with your significant other about the way you have treated them. Remember, this isn't necessarily the end of the relationship, but you will have to put in some work to learn how to change your behavior.

How to Leave with Children

If you have a child with an abuser, it can be emotional and complicated. It's a tough choice to take your children with you. Remember that children can suffer from emotional abuse, too. If the abuser isn't already abusing them also, they can feel and see the effects the emotional abuse has done to you.

Your abuser might threaten to take your children from you if you leave them. If your abuser has broken a lot of boundaries, you have probably already heard the threat. There are many tactics your abuser might use to place the child in between you. These might include turning the child against you, kidnapping, emotionally abusing the child or telling the state that you are unfit and have the child removed from the home.

You might be freaking out right now, but you have to know what to look for and expect when you are making plans to leave. Breathe. Relax. You have to create a safety plan. This is a plan of action you create that can help you figure out how to handle the situation and the right way to react to abusive situations.

Tell your children their job is to remain safe and it is not to try and protect you. Figure out a place where you can meet that is safe and make up a code word that will let them know when it's safe to leave the safe place. Tell them how and where they can go for help if they don't feel safe.

Pack an emergency bag for yourself and your child. Make sure to put in all their important papers. If you don't have a safe place to put it, leave it with a friend or somebody you trust. Know that there are shelters and family advocates that will give you advice and help you. If you don't know what resources are available in your town, visit the National Domestic Violence website. They have a chat available so you can talk with someone.

Memorize phone numbers and have your children memorize them too, if they are old enough, just in case you don't have a phone with you. Know that if you leave and take the children with you, you might have a custody battle in your future. You must speak with a lawyer to know your options. You don't want to break the law or remain on the run when you finally get away from your abuser.

Making a Safety Plan

For a person who is in an abusive relationship, it's important to make a safety plan. You can either memorize it or write it down. There are some steps you will need to take.

If your abuser emotionally abuses you, keep as much evidence as you can, like messages and emails. If the messages are threatening, make sure you don't delete them. Take pictures or print them up if you can.

Tell somebody you trust what is happening. You don't have to tell family or friends. Reach out to a professional who understands abusive relationships. When you tell somebody this, make sure you aren't the only one who knows about your problem.

Give the person or people you tell about your abuse copies of any threatening messages and emails if you can. As I started seeking help escaping from my abusive ex, this was one of the most valuable pieces of advice I received from a fellow abuse survivor. She told me about how her abusive ex-husband had tried to fight her request for a restraining order in a court as well as tried to get custody of their children, claiming that she was mentally unstable and making all of the abuse accusations up. He had sent her threatening emails but had been careful not to send anything over the phone, so she only had the emails for proof. He had found out where she lived, located her physical and digital copies of the emails, and destroyed them. Thankfully, she had given copies of threatening emails—which ranged from threats of sexual assault to threatening to kill both of them and their children—to a couple counselors at the women's shelter, and they were able to present that to the judge for the restraining order and the custody case.

After hearing that story, I made sure to give printed copies of all messages and emails to the counselors at the women's shelter and, later on, my psychiatrist. Keep your own copies but also make sure there are backups so that there will be a solid, irrefutable paper trail.

If at all possible, try to set money aside. If you have an abuser that controls the finances, this might be hard. Ask friends, family, or someone you trust to hold on to your money.

When you leave, be sure you take important documents with you like your identification. It would be a good idea to make a copy of all of them, too. The deed to your home, marriage license, work permits, and medical records need to be copied and kept safe.

When you leave your abuser, change up your habits. Change your phone number, switch work schedules. Never stay in the same routine that your abuser knows. Think about renting a post office box for your mail so your abuser can't keep track of you. If you take a restraining order out on your abuser, keep a copy on you at all times.

It's vital that when you have removed yourself from your abuser, you get emotionally supportive people around you. Remember that there will people, even people who should be close to you, who will be fooled by your abuser's act or will choose not to believe the truth. You do not need such people in your life as they will only weigh you down with doubt and negativity. Surround yourself with those who will believe you, help you, and support you.

Set goals for yourself that you know you can achieve. Stay focused on your recovery.

Be nice to yourself. When you come from an emotionally abusive situation, it is easy to forget that you have to be gentle and kind to yourself, too. Take time to heal and know that you are worthy.

If you are a loved one or friend to someone who is being abused, your best plan is to just be supportive. Help them connect with resources and just listen. Don't give their information or location to anybody or on social media. Helping someone you love can be hard when they don't do everything you want them to. You have to be patient. Everybody processes abuse in their own way.

Basically, you are the only one who can decide if their controlling behavior is something you want to put up with or not. Relationships need to support your growth and not diminish it. Love will celebrate you and never put you down. You deserve a loving and powerful relationship. You have to begin with yourself. You have to love yourself enough to take the first steps to reclaim yourself.

Many couples will deal with problems with control. It is a normal tension that comes up from time to time. If you or a loved one is struggling with ways to deal with the problem constructively, never hesitate to reach out. There are people who care and want to help.

Chapter 10: Finding Closure with Your Abuser

I wasted more time than I'd like to admit pining for closure with my ex. If I hadn't been so afraid of him, I probably would've been calling him constantly trying to achieve it. Looking back, I know I never would've gotten any closure from him, and any attempt to get it would have only weakened or reversed any progress I had made in healing. It might have even sucked me back into that cycle of abuse, especially if he found out where I was living.

The sad truth is that most of us won't ever be able to find closure with our abusers. Why?

Most of them don't want to give it.

To give closure to their victim would mean admitting that they did something wrong. They would have to admit that the abuse occurred in the first place. They won't want to fess up to anything that makes them look bad, let alone *that*.

Now, some of them might do that; some of them might realize that they have a problem and genuinely want to work to get better, so they will admit to their wrongdoing. Many won't.

If your relationship is with a narcissistic, sociopathic, or psychopathic abuser, it's almost guaranteed that they won't acknowledge it. True to form, they'll just turn it around on you and gaslight you, as we've already discussed. If you can't even get them to admit there was abuse, you'll never get closure from them.

They also won't want to surrender their power over you, and that is exactly what they would be doing by helping you get closure in your relationship. To give you closure would be to allow you to move on with your life. They would be letting both of you know that they don't have power over you anymore. Again, some of them might realize that they are troubled and will give you this peace, but most of the time, it just doesn't happen.

Instead, you must find closure in yourself. The only way to do that is to focus on yourself, not your abuser, and on your recovery. Once I began to truly process my experience and focused on reclaiming my own life rather than longing for some

certificate of resolution from my ex, I found that
I was finally able to move on. I could start to be
myself again.

Chapter 11: Recovery Stages

If you have ever been in a relationship that was emotionally abusive, there is a lot that has to be processed. People might remain in these relationships for many years. It is hard to imagine the amount of abuse that is endured in that amount of time. It is sad to say that it is a lot. Living through this type of traumatic experience can have a negative impact on a person's self-esteem.

Both genders can be subjected to emotional abuse in intimate relationships. It doesn't matter whether the abuse was done by or to females or males; the people who experience it get damaged deeply. The capacity to protect oneself in future relationships will be damaged along with their sense of worth if they don't heal correctly.

This abuse is hard on your spirit and mind. If you have left the abusive relationship, congratulations, you've done something that takes a lot of courage. If you are still in the abusive relationship, don't kick yourself and know that it is very difficult to leave this type of relationship. Things

will change. You will get better. When you can figure out a way that is safe to leave the relationship,
you will then be about to heal, and this is what is
important. The first step is figuring a way out to
get out. The second step is to heal the wounds.

It doesn't matter if the abuse was from your childhood or from an adult relationship. Victims of
emotional abuse usually suffer a lot of symptoms
that can be self-destructive. The physical and
emotional aspects of these symptoms are very
similar to those of PTSD, like feeling helpless and
isolated, startle responses, guilt, blame, anxiety,
disturbing body reactions, flashbacks, nightmares, and upsetting and disturbing memories.

An abusive relationship is not your real life. You
aren't stuck with this life and you can leave whenever you want to. If you are afraid to leave, there
are resources out there to help you. The important thing to remember is to connect with
yourself. When you are subjected to emotionally
abusive relationships, you tend to forget who you
really are. You will lose sight because your abuser
will teach you to think that you aren't worth a

dime even though this isn't true. It is hard to look through all the lies the abuser has created.

Because of this, people who have experienced emotional abuse have problems finding a partner who isn't abusive. Their prior interactions cause them to be suspicious that any person would treat them with kindness and respect. Believing that there isn't anything better out there might cause them to choose the same type of partner over and over.

Their self-esteem might have diminished to a point where they feel unworthy, and this is a hurtful place. They have to remember that none of this has to do with you and it shows that the person who abuses them isn't well. They have low self-esteem, and this gets projected onto you and others.

People can't heal from trauma until the abuse has stopped. This can be done by leaving the relationship or by challenging their abuser. This is a lot easier said than done. Most victims have been so traumatized and brainwashed that they are too scared to challenge their partner and can't see a way out.

Once you have gotten out of the relationship, you have to remember the real you. You are now free from the ties that bound you to this person. Think of all the things you love about yourself. Think back to the way your life was before the relation-ship. What made you excited for life? What did you do for fun? What were your hobbies?

Even if you manage to get out of an abusive rela-tionship, it will still be an uphill battle to heal yourself. When you are away from all the abuse, you have to learn how to pick a better partner. You also need to constantly practice the struggle to keep healthy boundaries.

There are going to be triggers that will come up from the old relationship from time to time. You need to address them immediately. It is best to work on these things with a therapist. Don't repress or ignore them. Suppressing your triggers will make you feel a lot worse. It's important that you can be honest about the pain so you can heal from the abusive relationship.

Most victims of chronic abuse usually attract partners who are abusers. They only respond to the positive traits of this new prospective partner. Once they are in the relationship, they might continue to ignore the abusive signs because they desperately want to believe the goodness of their partner will outweigh the bad.

Many couples face problems where either one or both are trying to heal from past abuse in their current relationship or in a new one. Each person in the partnership has to be willing to change their abusive interaction. In a new relationship, they know that there are always triggers present that need to be challenged and honored if they come up.

Emotionally abused people find that they need to change in their current relationship. They have to learn new responses that will help them heal while being triggered in their old ways.

Getting strength throughout the process will have better outcomes. People who can become powerful in their relationship are actively taking charge of their lives. Just like a person recovering from alcoholism who becomes calm when in a bar, they will see any abusive interaction as the time to practice and, in turn, strengthen their commitment.

For this to happen, abuse survivors have to pick a partner who will support and understand their journey and will stay with them through the stages of the process. If their partner is also a trauma survivor, they both have to trust each other to participate in the complicated exchanges. Couples who can do this through therapy will create a relationship that will be admired by others.

There are four stages to healing from abuse in a relationship. Since it is a challenging and difficult process, some can't make it through all of them. Even if only parts of them are done, they will get better in future relationships.

Here are the four stages of healing abuse:

1. Acknowledging the abuse

You can't heal what you can't see. Most abuse victims feel terrified, shamed, or humiliated when they bring up their traumatic experiences, not to mention how they feel when they share them with their significant others. Most of them were taught by the abuser that they are responsible for all the punishment they lived through, especially the sexual abuse. They have been brainwashed to think they willingly participated and benefited from the experience.

Most victims don't want to relive their past. They believe if they don't think about the abuse, it will magically go away. It might be unconscious to them because they had to bury it in order to survive. They become aware of the abuse after their partner's behavior triggers them.

Many victims put themselves down by ignoring their reactions as if they fantasized about them, were out of line, exaggerated, or were overly dramatic. Since they haven't experienced true love, they easily accept negative experiences instead of positive ones, and this traps them into more abuse. Some say when they share their abuse with new partners, it results in them being viewed as "damaged" and aren't worth fighting for.

When trauma is acknowledged to the partner and self, the healing can start. Remembering the abuse is painful, but knowing their partners will listen to them and make them feel safe during the process shows them the injustice that has happened to them.

While opening up wounds, the victims feel their emotions just like the abuse is happening all over again. They might feel alone, beaten, hopeless, trapped, angry, or helpless even if they are with their new partner. While the feelings emerge, they might try to project their abuser onto their new partner as an abuser even if they haven't behaved in that way.

It is crucial that their new partner know not to take those expressions personally and remain non-defensive and centered. This isn't easy and is actually difficult if their new partner has been abused, too.

2. Determined to save yourself

This is the "make it or break it" challenge. The victim has to take a stand no matter what. You have to preserve yourself in the presence of any trigger or threat, even if you have to turn off being aware of their needs, feelings, or thoughts.

This stance is going to be new to the victim and can come across to their partner as being indifferent. Self-serving, selfish, pulled-back, threatening, armored, dramatic, reactive, and startled responses explode and might threaten a relationship without any warning.

If you don't know how to balance self-preservation with caring and compassion for your partner, the healing will err toward survival, even if they don't realize they have hurt and distanced the people who are important to the process of healing.

It's only when the non-guilty, self-preserving, and self-protective partner finds peace with their new power that you can begin the next step. The emerging victor will never let themselves be abused or dominated. All the terror, resentment, and anger go away as the transformation becomes permanent.

Crucial point: In this stage, a break-up might be inevitable. It takes a very supportive, confident, and chivalrous partner to not take this stuff personally and to push back with their own needs. The battle will then become internal for the victim. Do they give up their heroic stance of taking care of oneself at all costs to meet the demands of others?

The victim doesn't have any choice but to continue on their path to preserve themselves, even if their partner sees it as selfish. It is helpful if the victim can acknowledge the problem without feeling the pressure to give up what has to be done.

3. Compassion

People who have gotten themselves out from under the tyranny can feel the new power in their lives, but now, they can feel compassion toward other victims and themselves.

They have given up living on a "witness stand" feeling, like they have to constantly defend or explain themselves. They have to beg and plead for mercy. They have figured out how to make others accountable for their actions and don't see the hard times as being their fault.

They have replaced guilt with trusting in their own change. They can see the trauma in others and not feel like they "have" to fix them.

They know they have to always watch for their internal abuser that has caused them to act the way they do. People who have been chronically abused were taught to divide the world between victims and abusers without having any other options. Now they are able to see the world outside these limits. They have triumphed over that voice that loves to abuse.

If they meet someone who triggers an old response, they need to make sure they don't feel cornered but investigate what lies beyond the person's agendas and motivations. They can do this with confidence. They know they won't allow themselves to get pulled into the trap of self-doubt.

Now that they feel like the master of their fate, they can choose why, when, how, and who they will love. They know what triggers bring them anguish, ways to recognize when it occurs, and how to change old reactions with strength. They know what they can offer, what they won't stand for, and what they are in need of in a way that only people why have recovered from trauma can.

4. Model for other people

The best way to learn is to teach others. The only warning is you have to teach by example and never by preaching. Once you are into the third stage, you will see yourself in two ways: The first will be in your behaviors and thoughts. You won't be attracted by or attracted to people who feel like they have to save their victims or are abusive. You will have more compassion for damaging relationships, and you won't feel obligated to fix or join them.

The second one is the people who are around you now will treat you with respect. They want to know how you changed from a victim into a warrior. You get to tell them that you broke free from the bonds of your abuser and you are now a model for others who need help.

Chapter 12: Reclaiming Your Life

Many people spend most of their lives avoiding isolation, cold shoulders, put-downs, anger, resentment, and criticism. They get used to behaving and thinking how everybody thinks they should that it becomes hard for them to even realize what is best for them and what they believe. They have tried many times to create harmony, but every time, they second-guess themselves on matters both small and large until they have lost sight of who they really are.

If this description fits you, you need to get reacquainted with your inner self. Don't worry; this process is actually very pleasant. It is like seeing an old friend from childhood and taking time to catch up. The only difference is that you aren't getting to know an old friend; you are getting to know yourself on a deeper level while discovering your inner self.

Some aspects of our inner self we get from our cultural influences, the others we learn from life experiences. There are others that come from our inner values.

Temperament

This is a mix of genetic traits. It is partially the product of a person's metabolism, or the way our bodies create energy. Temperament is thought to be a type of "emotional tone," or the way it feels being you.

Each human and animal is born with their own temperament. Scientists have combined areas of measurement into several categories that we have termed as characteristics. Some of them get presented on a continuum such as aggressive – sociable, fearless – fearful, outgoing – shy. A sensory threshold is one aspect of temperament. This means a person could become easily bored or over-stimulated. Average energy level refers to how easily a person can mentally and physically do a task. The average level of arousal refers to how excited a person can get.

Using these aspects, you can begin your journey of discovering yourself. Just like any psychological classification, these don't tell us much about the actual person. If you were to give birth to four children, you will have four separate temperaments. Each of your children will be their own person even if they share many characteristics and traits with their siblings and parents.

Adaptation

The way a person adapts to their temperamental qualities can account for the differences we can see in their personalities. Basically, a person can't change their temperament. A child who is easily excitable will grow into an adult who is easily excitable. What we can do is adapt our temperaments in numerous ways. People who were easily excitable as children learn with time how to manage their arousal levels. If they choose healthy adaptations, they will be able to enjoy their temperaments without hindering their limitations.

If you are shy, you have realized growing up that you were never the life of the party, but you probably learned how to enjoy and contribute to the party by focusing and paying attention to others. You might have beaten yourself up when you were younger about being shy, but you learned how to overcome and adapt. If you don't have a lot of energy, you know you won't ever be a marathon runner or sprinter, but you might have learned to increase your energy by taking brisk walks regularly. If you have a low persistence level, you can boost your confidence in several different ways, but you have to let yourself make mistakes. This removes emotional blocks, but you will still have the impulse to just give up. Many of our impulses won't become an overt behavior because we can learn to regulate them by utilizing routines.

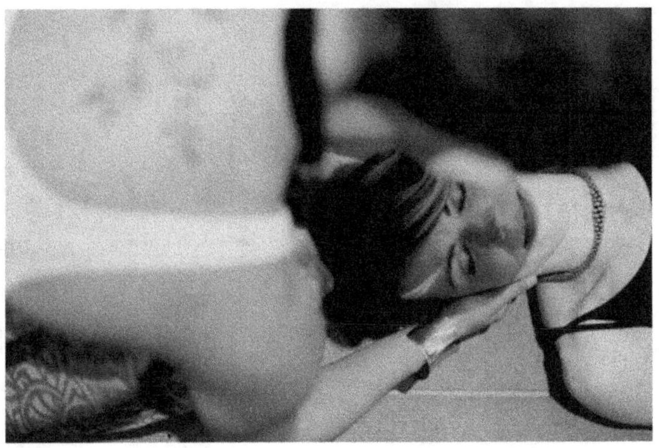

Even though many of our temperamental adaptations happen without us knowing it, or by trial and error, we can alter them deliberately if we want to. If you constantly pay attention to detail, you need to step back occasionally to get a look at the big picture. If you have a low interest level, you have to dig deep into things to keep your interest. If you are always positive or negative, know that you won't be able to trust your gut instinct when entering new situations or meeting new people.

You have the ability to make as many adaptations to your temperament as you need to if you honor and respect what is in your genes.

Self-Care Practices

When someone who has been emotionally abused gets out of a toxic relationship, their healing journey has just begun. These victims are still going to feel symptoms of trauma like feeling worthless, depression, dissociation, anxiety, nightmares, and recurring flashbacks. They could also feel like they need to reconnect or check in with their abuser because of trauma bonds that were created during the abuse.

Getting help from a therapist who specializes in trauma abuse and learning some self-care practices are great ways to learn how to tend to your spirit, body, and mind.

Every healing method isn't going to work for everyone, so you need to experiment with the following to find the ones that work best for your journey. These can be very beneficial for your healing. These practices have the potential to save your life on your journey to recovery:

1. Exercise

Having a daily exercise routine could save your life. Find something that you enjoy doing and do it daily. It could be swimming, running, walking, dancing, whatever; just get up and move. If you don't have a lot of motivation, begin small. Start off by committing to 30 minutes of walking instead of running. When you exercise, it lowers cortisol levels and releases endorphins. It replaces the addictions we developed with our abuses and gives us a better outlet.

Exercise lets you embody your strength and resilience after you leave your abuser. It can help you battle the biochemical addiction that your body developed during the abuse.

This addiction is caused by chemicals such as serotonin, adrenaline, cortisol, and dopamine that exaggerate the bond to the abuser during the lows and highs of the abuse. Exercise can start countering the side effects of the abuse like illness, sleeping disorders, premature aging, and weight gain that are caused by our immune system being overwhelmed by trauma.

2. Sleep

Being well-rested is essential for your mental well-being. Depression, anxiety, stress, and trauma can all throw off people's sleep patterns. Sometimes it gives them nightmares. Other times, they can't fall asleep at night. Still other times, they can't manage to stay awake. At the same time, not getting enough sleep can also make depression, anxiety, stress, and trauma even worse, creating a vicious cycle that will only send you into a downward spiral.

You must make sure you get enough sleep, normally 7-9 hours a night, depending on the individual. Get to bed around the same time every night and set an alarm to get up the same time every morning. If you're having any difficulties with sleeping, talk to your primary care physician.

3. Meditation

When you have been traumatized, the areas in the brain that are related to functioning such as focus, regulating emotions, planning, memory, and learning get disrupted. Meditation has been proven to help certain areas of the brain like the hippocampus, amygdala, and the prefrontal cortex.

Mediation puts the survivor back into the driver's seat. It gives the ability to heal their brain and reclaim their reality from empowerment instead of trauma.

Daily meditation can strengthen neural pathways positively. It can increase grey matter in the brain that relates to regulating emotions and diminishes the flight-or-fight response that goes a bit crazy during trauma. Meditation makes you more aware of your cravings to have contact with your abuser and allows you to be more mindful of your emotions. This gives you space to think about alternatives before you act impulsively and go back to the toxic relationship.

4. Anchoring

Emotional abuse survivors have usually been gaslighted into believing the abuse wasn't real. You need to anchor yourself back to reality instead of idealizing the relationship. This is helpful for survivors when they start to question how real the abuse was or if they have mixed emotions about their abusers who only show affection just to keep them in the abusive relationship. Most victims

have positive emotions toward their abusers because of techniques such as intermittent rein-
forcement and love bombing. Other survivors
might associate them to survival if the abuse
threatened their physical and emotional safety.

Anchoring helps you reconnect to the reality that
the abuser tried to destroy. It gives the survivor
validation and reduces cognitive discord about
the true identity of the abuser.

Survivors are very vulnerable once they leave the
toxic relationship. The abuser will try to trick
them into coming back by putting on their false
albeit sweet persona. This is why it is essential to
block all phone calls and text messages from your
abuser. You also have to get rid of all the connec-
tions you have with them and their enablers on all
social media. This will get rid of all information
and temptation about them. It gives the survivor
a clean slate where they can reconnect to the truth
about what happened and the way they felt instead of the way the abuser distorts the situation.

To start anchoring yourself, make a list of the ten
worst incidents that happened during the rela-

tionship or ten ways the abuser made you feel degraded. This will be useful when you get tempted to reach out to them, respond to an attempt to get you back, or look them up.

It would be best to work with a therapist to make this list so you can get help with any triggers that might come up when trying to anchor yourself. If there are incidents that you find horribly triggering, it might be best to pick ones that aren't as triggering until you can manage your emotions in healthy ways.

If you can learn to make statements like "My abuser disrespected me daily" or "They made me feel small each time I succeeded," they can help you remember if you start rationalizing, denying, or minimizing the abuse. It can be difficult to redirect your focus to all the abuse within the relationship, but it can help reduce cognitive discord about the abuser. Reducing cognitive discord is necessary for your recovery.

5. Yoga

If you are feeling the effects of the trauma in your body, it would be great to use an activity that combines physical activity and mindfulness to help bring empowerment and restore balance. Yoga can help ease anxiety and depression. It can improve symptoms of PTSD, bolster self-esteem, expand emotional regulation skills, and improve body image.

Yoga lets abuse survivors counter the powerlessness they feel from the trauma that gets stored in the body by engaging in powerful movements. Yoga can provide self-mastery that helps you regain ownership of your body. It lets survivors rebuild their sense of safety that trauma takes away from them. It can also get rid of the feeling of disassociation by reconnecting them to their body.

6. Creative Pursuits

Creativity is a great outlet for trauma and can have a very soothing effect overall. Creative pursuits allow abuse survivors to express those emotions that they have had to suppress for so long and control and manipulate them in ways that they lost the ability to when they entered the relationship with their abuser. Sometimes it's even an activity that they used to enjoy but that the abuser belittled or told them they were no good at, and picking it up again will be symbolic of taking back the life that the abuser had ripped away from them.

It doesn't really matter which creative pursuit you prefer—music, art, writing, dance, making collages, so forth—or even if you're any good at it. So long as you enjoy it, it will help you to get connected with your emotions and your inner self. Additionally, just completing a creative project also will give you a sense of accomplishment that will raise your self-esteem, even if nobody else will ever see it. If you find happen to find out that you also have a knack for it, that will be a happy bonus.

7. Spend Time with Animals

When I was living in America, I had a friend who went to university in Northern California. She said that there was a program on the campus where every month, volunteers brought trained dogs to the quad specifically for the purpose of being petted and played with by students. The idea was that doing so was supposed to help ease the students' stress levels, especially around finals. According to my friend, it worked, at least for her. But she wasn't just suffering from stress related to school; she also suffered from depression and anxiety after years of emotional abuse that both she and her mother had to endure from her father. The dogs, she told me, helped to calm her and get her open a bit, which allowed her to regain some of the control over her emotions that she never had as a child.

The unconditional, unjudging love of an animal can warm even the coldest hearts. That's why animal-assisted therapy has been introduced into more hospitals and treatment centers lately, to help everyone from child cancer patients and elderly people with dementia to veterans with

PTSD and people with depression. You might not be able to get a pet yourself or even visit a medical center that offers animal-assisted therapy, but perhaps you could spend the afternoon with a friend's dog or pet-sit your sister's cat. You could even visit the local dog park and see if any of the owners will let you pet their dogs—just always remember to ask first. If they say no, respect that. There's always a reason.

8. Talk with a Counselor

In dealing with my abusive ex, I mostly visited counselors as a way to leave a record of the abuse to help me get out. When it came to my emotional struggles during the relationship and after I left him, I turned to a psychiatrist. However, I've spoken with many women who've found that just talking with a counselor has done wonders for them.

I must emphasize here that a counselor will *not* give you prescriptions for any medication. Psychiatrists can as they are medical doctors, but mental health counselors are not licensed to do so. If you are someone who would just like to talk to an impartial third party and get the tools to help you move forward and heal from your situation, then counseling or psychotherapy might be able to help you. Finding a counselor could especially be helpful if you have found those around you are either having a hard time accepting the truth about your abuse or are unwilling to help you through it. It's a bitter reality, but it can happen, and when it does, it's nice to have someone to turn to.

9. Write a Letter to Your Younger Self

Just like acknowledging the abuse happened is crucial to recovering, being able to forgive yourself for it happening in the first place is crucial for reclaiming your life. When you look back on the abuse, you might be mad at yourself. You might think that all the signs were there, that you were too passive and therefore allowed yourself to be abused. But you have to remember that hindsight is 20/20. Everything seems obvious when you look back on it later. What you need to do is not be mad at yourself because this happened. More than that, you need to forgive yourself for it happening. Otherwise, you'll never be able to reclaim your life. It's like when you're mad at a friend at can't start talking to them again until you talk through things and one or both of you apologize. You need to talk things through with your younger self and forgive yourself.

To this end, write a letter to your younger self. Talk about everything that has happened since the abuse began. It'll be painful, but try to get through it in one sitting if you can. Just let it all out: the frustration, the belittlement, the isolation, the hurt. Then talk about where you're going from here, how things will be better now. Most importantly, remind yourself that this wasn't your fault and tell yourself that you forgive yourself for not being able to stop it sooner. Read this last part out loud if you have to. You might feel silly doing this at first, but after you've been at it a while, you'll be getting more and more into it emotionally and mentally. By the end, you might not fully be at peace with yourself, but at least you'll finally realize that even though the signs were there does not mean you could have done anything. You can finally accept this was not your fault and start to reclaim the life you had before the abuse.

10. Working with the Inner Child

Even though you were traumatized by an abuser, there might have been other traumas that were brought about because of the relationship. You might have a wounded inner child that needs to be helped by your adult self when you feel emotional. Unmet childhood needs were aggravated by the experience; self-compassion is needed during your healing journey.

Survivors often struggle with self-blame and toxic shame after being abused. They know logically that they had no control over the abuse, but the abuse can bring up old wounds that never got healed. It can cause a bigger pattern of always feeling like they're never good enough. Changing the way you talk to yourself is critical when healing. It tackles old narratives that have been cemented in the brain.

Being gentle with yourself is crucial after abuse. The most powerful type of compassion is self-compassion.

If these deep-seated, ancient emotions come up, try to soothe yourself just like you were talking to somebody you truly love. Write some positive affirmations down that you can say to yourself when you are grieving like: "I am worthy of love and respect" or "I deserve peace." This will help you learn to exhibit understanding and sensitivity to yourself that curbs self-blame and self-judgment. Self-compassion extends to keeping no contact, too.

When you blame and judge yourself, you will engage in self-sabotage since you don't think you are worthy of joy, stability, and peace. Once you accept that you are going to show compassion toward yourself, you need to remind yourself that you are worthy of kindness and care.

There is an empowering and victorious life in front of you after abuse. You can thrive and survive, but you have to commit to self-care.

Suicide Prevention

It's not a comfortable topic, but it is a necessary one. As I explained earlier in this book, emotional abuse can reach the point that the victim might contemplate suicide. Even after leaving your abuser, you might reach a low point in your life before your recovery begins. If this happens, don't be afraid to reach out. Talk to loved ones not involved with your abuser—or, at least, who you know won't tell your abuser about any of this. Talk to your primary care physician or even a therapist. If you feel these thoughts bearing down on you, call the hotline number provided in the "Helpful Resources" section of this book.

You are more than what your abuser has made you. You will survive this.

Chapter 13: Guided Journal

To help you start your healing journey, here you will find a guided journal. This journal will help you to work through your thoughts and feelings. A lot of change will take place in your life during recovery, and it's nice to have a place to write things down. Please keep in mind, if you are still in the abusive relationship, to keep you journal in a safe place where your abuser cannot find it. This is for your safety.

What Happened Today (quickly jot down everything you remember from the day):

How did you feel when you got up?

How do you feel right now?

Write Down a Happy Memory (this could be from today or any day):

Fill in the blanks using your happy memory:

"I remember feeling good when_________________________. I felt _________________________ [use a few words to describe how you felt]. I was _____________ [location], and

I remember ___________ [a sensory feeling]. It was during a time when I was ___________________ [a general description or activity]. I won't ever forget _____________________ [describe the people, environment, etc.] around me. I won't get to be in the exact same setting again, but I know I can feel that again."

How do you want to feel tomorrow?

One Last Reminder Before Conclusion

Have you grabbed your free resource?

A lot of information has been covered in this book. As previously shared, I've created a simple mind map that you can use *right away* to easily understand, quickly recall and readily use what you've learned in this book.

If you've not grabbed it…

Click Here To Get Your Free Resource

Alternatively, here's the link:

https://viebooks.club/freeresourcemind-mapforemotionalabuserecovery

Conclusion

Thank for making it through to the end of this book. Let's hope it was informative and able to provide you with all the tools you need in order to remove and overcome emotional abuse.

You will likely hit a few bumps along your journey of healing, but you'll work through them. Nothing worthwhile is ever easy, keep that in mind. If you are currently in an emotionally abusive relationship, the first thing you need to do is find a way out and make sure that you are safe. I understand this is no easy feat, but it's important for your wellbeing.

Find people you can trust. They will be your anchors in your recovery, the safe place you can come to when you need help. Stick with your journey of recovery and you will be living a life that you never imagined was possible. You can do this, I have faith in you.

Sincerely,

Marjorie Lise

P.S.

If you've found this book helpful in any way, a review on Amazon is greatly appreciated.

This means a lot to me, and I'll be extremely grateful.

Helpful Resources

To make sure you can find help whenever you need it, here are some resources that can be useful should you need them:

Rape, Abuse, and Incest National Network: 1-800-656-HOPE

Substance Abuse and Mental Health Services Administration: https://findtreatment.samhsa.gov/

Help for male survivors: https://malesurvivor.org/

US National Domestic Violence Hotline: +1-800-799-7233

Yes I Can: http://yesican.org/

Suicide Hotline: 1-800-273-8255

Notes

[1] Glaser, Danya. "Emotional abuse and neglect (psychological maltreatment): a conceptual framework." *Elsevier* (2002): 697-714

[2] Karakurt Ph.D, Gunner and Kristen Silver B.A. "Emotional abuse in intimate relationships: The role of gender and age." *Violence and Victims* (2013): 804-821

[3] Ireland, JL and P Birch. "Emotionally abusive behavior in young couples: exploring a role for implicit aggression." *Violence and Victims* (2013): 656-659

[4] Norman, Rosana, et al. "The long-term health consequences of child physical abuse, emotional abuse, and neglect: A systematic review and meta-analysis." *PLOS: Medicine* (2012)

[5] Gass, Gertrude and William Nichols. "Gaslighting: A marital syndrome." *Contemporary Family Therapy* (1988): 3-16

[6] Carroll, Judith E., Tara L. Gruenewald, Shelley E. Taylor, Denise Janicki-Deverts, Karen A.

Matthews, and Teresa E. Seeman. "Childhood abuse, parental warmth, and adult multisystem biological risk in the Coronary Artery Risk Development in Young Adults study." *PNAS* (2013), 110 (42): 17149-17153

Related Books That Might Benefit You

Did My Narcissistic Mother Love Me?: Dealing with Manipulation & Trauma from Narcissist - Healing & Recovery of Narcissism Abuse in Toxic, Abusive Family Relationship with Parents, Mother or Father

Discover The PROVEN, Most Effective Ways To Heal From Abusive, Narcissistic Mothers & FINALLY Thrive In Life & Relationships!

Are you feeling overwhelming resentment and anger towards your narcissistic mother and some of your family members?

Do you struggle with regulating your emotions and letting other people in?

Do you feel frustrated because you can't seem to find a way to heal from your emotional wounds and establish healthy, loving relationships with others?

If you want to stop all these in your life, then keep reading...

One of the most difficult things for wounded children to accept is the fact that there is a very small chance that their narcissistic mothers will ever change. At best, they will look for ways to address their toxic traits and grow for the better. However, narcissists <u>*rarely change*</u>... and if they do start acting nicer, more often than not, it's because they seek to manipulate.

Award-winning author and narcissistic abuse survivor, Nanette Abigail, knows a thing or two about this sensitive issue. Her own

experience with getting out of a controlling relationship with her mother equipped her with the
insider knowledge, that had allowed her to finally
wake up to the reality that the problem wasn't
her, and that what she went through wasn't her
fault.

In her book, Abigail lays out the crucial tools she
used to set boundaries, create safe havens, and
find mental clarity for herself... and with her help,
you can, too!

***Did My Narcissistic Mother Love Me?*, the
only book you'll ever need to heal and
move forward with life after suffering
emotional turmoil from narcissistic parents.**

Here's a taste of what you'll discover inside *Did My Narcissistic Mother Love Me?*:

- *7 Essential facts adult daughters*
  with a narcissistic family need to be aware
  of, so they can FINALLY see and accept the
  hard truth

- ***Expert-approved methods to identify that VITAL moment*** your Psychological Immune System starts kicking in and field-tested ways to effectively boost it

- ***Eye-opening insights to understand WHY*** you grieve for the loving mother you never had, so you can finally start to overcome your negative emotions and destructive attachment

- ***Important first steps to kick off the process of healing*** from the toxic, narcissistic relationship you have with your abusive mother

- ***Proven ways to deal with your anger***, so you can clearly understand the reality of the situation you were in as you start your narcissistic abuse recovery

- ***Foolproof techniques to skillfully detach from and set healthy boundaries*** with a mother consumed with narcissism

- ***Practical tips in maximizing healing benefits*** of mindfulness as you recover from your abusive parents

And much, much more...

If you're ready to finally learn how to deal with,
set healthy boundaries, heal from your narcissistic mother, and say goodbye to the overwhelming
feelings of helplessness, now is the time.

Co-Dependency: The Crazy Codependent in Toxic Relationship - The Codependency Cure, Healing & Recovery from Trauma for Emotionally Healthy Love Relationships with Partner, Parent, Mother or Father

<u>This POWERFUL Guide Will Help You Overcome & Recover From Codependent Relationship & Cultivate Your Own Growth!</u>

Do you often feel guilty when you're not able to help someone who completely depends on you?

Are you feeling like you don't have the freedom to explore opportunities for growth?

Do you feel like you can't live up to your full potential because you have to take care of everyone's needs before your own?

If you want to stop all these in your life, then keep reading...

A codependent relationship can feel like a burden on the person bearing the brunt of other people's problems. Being in it often leave you feeling used, unappreciated and angry. Most times, you feel almost forced to help certain people solve their problems as you feel compelled to pacify their negative emotions, give various suggestions, or offer unwanted advice.

Margot Fayre, Doctor of Psychology, knows this all too well. Once in a codependent relationship herself, she knows how frustrating and limiting all of this can feel like. This was the impetus that drove her to write her book, so she can help people like you overcome codependency using science-backed insights.

Are you ready to find out if you're being taken advantage of, end your codependent relationship, and finally set yourself free?

Co-Dependency, the only book you'll ever need to finally overcome and recover from a codependent partner, friend or relative who hampers your growth, and start cultivating emotionally healthy relationships.

Here's a taste of what you'll discover inside *Co-Dependency*:

- ***Definitely understand what it means to be in a codependent relationship*** so you can make the necessary life changes using SIMPLE techniques

- ***Quickly discover what your triggers are*** so you know how your mind works and EASILY put an end to your codependence issues

- ***Firmly set your personal boundaries*** and COURAGEOUSLY assert yourself so you no longer need to depend on anybody

- **_Effectively make changes within_** using mindfulness and practical methods based on PROVEN psychology principles

- **_Take absolute, full responsibility for your own emotions_** and resolve conflicts using FIELD-TESTED methods

- **_Fast-track your journey in recovering from co-dependency_** by figuring out and tapping into your GREATEST strengths

- **_Become a better partner, friend and family member_** by becoming a GREAT team player and advocate

And much, much more...

If you're ready to finally take back control of your life, live up to your maximum potential, and say goodbye to your controlling relationships, now is the time.

Narcissistic Abuse Recovery in Toxic Relationship: Healing Love & Recovering from Covert Narcissism, Manipulation & Trauma - Dealing with Abusive Narcissist Partner, Family, Parent, Mother or Father

<u>This LIFE-CHANGING Guide Will Teach You How To Cut Narcissist Out Of Your Life So They Can Never Hurt You Again!</u>

Do you often feel like you're condoning abusive behavior from people who claim to love you?

Have you stopped doing the things you love because someone in your life criticizes you for doing them?

Do you feel suffocated and overwhelmed because you are under constant undeserved scrutiny?

If you want to stop all these in your life, then keep reading...

Dealing with narcissists can be emotionally and psychologically exhausting and traumatic. Most narcissists feel entitled to everyone's attention, as well as exploit others without guilt or shame. Often times, the victims never really know what hit them until it's too late.

Award-winning author, Naila Farrah, knows a thing or two about falling victim to a narcissist. In fact, her experience was even more heartbreaking since the abuser was her own father — someone who is supposed to make her feel safe and loved. Once she had stopped condoning his bad behavior, her world changed for the better and this paved the way to her narcissistic abuse recovery. All of a sudden, it was like a heavy weight had been taken off her shoulders. She became happier, brighter, and content... and she wishes the same things for you, too!

In her book, Farrah aims to empower people like you to take back control and start living life free from toxic, controlling people.

***Narcissistic Abuse Recovery in Toxic Relationship*, the only book you'll ever need to discover the reality of covert narcissism and learn how to spot a narcissist with narcissistic personality disorder before they start hurting you!**

Here's a taste of what you'll discover inside *Narcissistic Abuse Recovery in Toxic Relationship*:

- ***Swiftly learn the signs to watch out for*** so you can SKILLFULLY stop a narcissist from coming into your life and creating chaos

- ***Easily find out if you're in a relationship with a narcissist*** so you can EFFECTIVELY deal with them and kick start your own narcissistic abuse recovery

- ***Effectively cut toxic people out of your life*** using this one FOOLPROOF method that will change the course of your life

- ***Fast-track your healing from a narcissistic relationship*** and get your life back in a snap using PROVEN techniques and tools

- ***Discover the exact ways*** you can QUICKLY heal your brain from all the emotional turmoil and trauma and reverse whatever damage has been done

- ***Use SCIENCE-BACKED, practical advice*** so you can FINALLY move forward and start a new life away from your narcissistic abuser

- ***Immediately free yourself*** from a narcissistic person's grip and start cultivating healthier relationships with a few SIMPLE steps

And much, much more...

If you're ready to finally learn how to deal with a narcissist, break free from the emotional and psychological chaos, start your narcissistic abuse recovery, and live a happier, contented and fulfilled life, now is the time.